A Blessed Human Life

Witness Lee

Living Stream Ministry

Anaheim, CA • www.lsm.org

First Edition, April 2003.

ISBN 0-7363-2277-9

Published by

Living Stream Ministry
2431 W. La Palma Ave., Anaheim, CA 92801 U.S.A.
P. O. Box 2121, Anaheim, CA 92814 U.S.A.

Printed in the United States of America

03   04   05   06   07   08   09   /   9   8   7   6   5   4   3   2   1

CONTENTS

PREFACE

This book is composed of messages given by Brother Witness Lee in Taipei, Taiwan in various conferences and the Full-Time Training during the 1980s. These messages were not reviewed by the speaker.

CHAPTER ONE

A BLESSED HUMAN LIFE

Scripture Reading: Heb. 11:24-26; Phil. 3:7-8, 12-14

Young people are precious. Having just begun their journey in life, they are full of youthful vigor and have a promising future. That is why everyone likes young people. Nevertheless, may the Lord have mercy on us that the young people can see what is truly a blessed human life.

HUMAN LIFE MEANING HUMAN EXISTENCE

Concerning a blessed human life, the emphasis is not just on being *blessed;* rather, the emphasis is on *human life.* Human life is our subject. What is human life? We all know that the phrase *human life* is composed of *human* and *life.* What is human? It is a mystery. As for life, its meaning is somewhat obscure. Does it refer to the intrinsic life or to the outward living? It seems to refer to both aspects and to also include both. Actually, this life is neither the intrinsic life nor the outward living; it lies between life and living and refers to human existence. Human life refers to the existence of man, and the existence of man is what man is. What we are is our real human life. In other words, our human life shows the secret of our being human.

A person begins to exist as soon as he is born. During the first two to three years, he knows only to eat, drink, and play; he does not understand anything else. As he grows up little by little, on the one hand, his taste for pleasure increases, but on the other hand, his gratification from pleasure decreases gradually. Today, especially in Taiwan, starting from kindergarten the human life seems to be a suffering life instead of a blessed life. The reason for this is that from the time of kindergarten, demands from teachers, expectations from parents, and the pressures of schoolwork all come one after another.

We who have children are well aware of this matter. After a child goes to kindergarten, teachers do everything they can to coax him to study diligently. After he passes through elementary school, he enters junior high, and in order to get a good education not only does the child suffer hardships in the school, but the parents also go to much trouble with the view that he would pass his examinations and enter into the best high school. The parents toil day and night and even provide him with the best tutor. Therefore, not only is the school strict in supervision, but the tutor also is not at all lax, and even the parents keep a close watch. At last he passes the test, but he is still not satisfied, for his scores may not be high enough to get him admitted to a first rate school; rather, he may be admitted to a second rate school. After entering into high school, he suffers even more because college is still ahead. After he enters college, there are still a few more years of suffering.

Just before graduating from college, or maybe even earlier, some may have heard the gospel, believed in Jesus, and received salvation, acquiring a priceless blessing. However, they may not understand why they believed. The reason they believed is that now they have a stronger will and a broader view, and as to human life and man's existence they have a deeper understanding. In other words, it is at this point in life that they begin to sense the need of a human being and the need of human life. Therefore, under the Lord's sovereignty and arrangement, they heard the gospel and received the Lord.

I believed in Jesus when I was nineteen years old. At that time I was still studying in a junior college. To tell you the truth, I had had my fill of fun and pleasure. My mother was a third generation Christian, so I was born and grew up in Christianity, and the school I attended was a Christian school. After I gradually became more mature, I constantly felt that I should make a stand for the Lord, since the Christian religion in China at that time was commonly referred to as a "foreign religion" in a derogatory way. Nevertheless, even at nineteen years of age, I had not yet received Christ. That was when my human life had come to the point where I was empty within and without. Even though I knew some principles of dealing with things and understood a little about human life, I was empty inside.

One afternoon, a young lady from the Kiangsu-Chekiang area of the South came into our city to preach the gospel. I grew up listening to sermons given by old pastors and old preachers, so I was weary of listening to them. Now there was a preacher who was not only a young person, but also a female, coming to our city to preach the gospel. Naturally I was driven by curiosity to go listen to her. That afternoon I went and heard her preaching. Right away, there was a response within me, and my heart felt that this was what I wanted. At that moment, I believed in the Lord. I remember that after the meeting that day, on my way back home, I stopped and looked up to the heavens and said, "O God, even if you give me the entire world today, I will not accept it. I only want You." It was not a so-called supplication but an aspiration. That year I had just entered junior college.

Apparently, we just hear the gospel and believe in Jesus, but actually it is not that simple; it is very deep. It is deep in the sense that it concerns our very being. Our existence comes to a point, a critical moment, when our state of mind is prepared to receive something; so when the gospel comes, we receive Jesus. This shows that our human existence is certainly for a purpose. Everything in the universe is for our existence. If all the beasts, birds, and cattle were taken away, human life would lose its color. All the lovely animals are part of our human life and they are for our existence. Therefore, we must consider what human life is exactly, what the meaning of human life is, and what the purpose of man's existence is.

THE WONDER OF THE CREATION OF MAN

If we were to stand in front of the mirror and look at ourselves—at our eyes, nose, and ears—we would find them fascinating. It is truly the wonderful design of the Creator that we human beings are such. No wonder someone once praised in admiration, saying, "Throughout history and over the whole earth, there is not one great designer who can improve the human appearance." Today the things in the world are wide in variety, diverse in style, and always being modified. Some are modified to improve their function; some are modified for fashion, to follow the tide of the age. Only we human beings cannot be improved either in appearance or in function. For example, if the eyebrows above our eyes were modified to line up vertically, they would be not only ugly but also impractical. In Taiwan, nine out of ten people wear glasses. If the nose God created for man was wide on the top and narrow on the bottom, not only would it not hold a pair of glasses, but it would also be ugly. If our nostrils were pointed upward, then all the dust and rain would fall into them. These illustrate that the creation of man is truly a wonder.

To illustrate further, the hairs on our body all grow downward, and only the hairs in the trachea grow upward. In this way the phlegm in the throat can be kept from flowing downward. A brother who is a medical doctor told me that the earwax in our ears is very useful medically; it instantly kills intruding bacteria, preventing them from doing any harm to us. Based on these things, we can conclude that human beings did not come through evolution as Darwin said. They were created by the sovereign Lord of the universe. Before creation there had to be a design; we were created according to the design of the wisdom of God. God's design is mysterious yet exquisite and cannot be further improved. We little human beings express God's great design to the uttermost.

THE MEANING OF HUMAN EXISTENCE

In this world there is not one designer who designs things without a purpose. In the same way, in the creation of man God also had an intention, a motive, and a purpose. According to this intention, motive, and purpose, He designed what He desired. This shows us that there is real meaning behind our human life and a reason for our existence. Since human beings were created according to God's design, what they are and the reason for their existence lie in the God who created them.

There are countless volumes of books, whether philosophical, literary, scientific, or religious, that have something to say about human existence. However, these discussions are incomplete, just like the proverbial blind man who tried to discern an elephant by feeling only one part of it. But in this vast sea of books, there is a book called the Bible. It begins with, "In the beginning God created the heavens and the earth" (Gen. 1:1). It also says that God made man in His image and according to His likeness (v. 26). Even though these words are easily understood, their implications are deep and profound. In short, man was created for and according to God's desire. God's creation is the basis of human existence. In other words, human existence came out of God's creation and also lies in God's creation, and it is entirely for the purpose of God's creation.

God did not create man without a basis; God made man in His image and according to His likeness. Although it is very difficult for us to describe God's image and likeness, the Bible portrays who God is in various ways. One of the portraits of God is the law in the Old Testament. In the Old Testament, the law is also called the testimony of God, that is, the "biography" of God. Apparently, the law is the Ten Commandments with many statutes plus many ordinances. However, after you read these commandments, statutes, and ordinances, you will come to a conclusion that the general principles of the law are love, light, holiness, and righteousness. Why do we say the law is the testimony of God? It is because the law that a person establishes is determined by the kind of person he is. God's law expresses the God who enacted this law.

In the New Testament, God says that He is love (1 John 4:8). He also says, "You shall be holy because I am holy" (1 Pet. 1:16). The teachings of the New Testament convey the spirit of the law; this is also the description of what God is. Therefore, the image of the unique God whom we worship is love, light, holiness, and righteousness. Man was created according to this image of God. Therefore, throughout history and over the whole earth, regardless of race or color, every human being has love within him. Even when he grows old, this essence of love still remains.

Furthermore, we all have light within; we like to be bright. We also have holiness within and like to be blameless and transcendent. We have righteousness within as well; we approve of fairness and justice. Even though we are fallen, we still retain the qualities of love, light, holiness, and righteousness, because God created us with these qualities. They are not obtained through education; as long as we are human beings, we have them. Love, light, holiness, and righteousness are the real and original inner content of all human beings. When a man expresses this inner content, he expresses his true nature.

Why did God create man according to His image? God's intention was that one day man might receive Him into him. When God created man, He created only a "framework"; man did not have God's divine life within him to live out the reality of love, light, holiness, and righteousness. It is when man receives God into him, when he prays to the Lord Jesus, calling His name, that man feels he is satisfied and that he has reality. He is at ease inwardly, and he can sleep well and eat well. Furthermore, now man has the power to live out God's substance of love, light, holiness, and righteousness.

Before we were saved, when we did not have the Lord, we were empty within. After we receive the Lord Jesus into us, we are filled inwardly. This is the meaning of human existence. Therefore, the existence of human beings is not for making money, obtaining a higher position, or having a golden future. The meaning of human existence lies in receiving our Creator, who is the real meaning of our life. This is human life. This God who is inside of us is our real blessing and our real joy. As a result, we become a blessed human being, and our existence becomes a blessed human life.

Today many have made a fortune in business, and many more have earned a college degree. Furthermore, more than a few have obtained a high position, success, and fame. However, the more successful a person is, the less God he may have and the emptier he will feel within. Young people have just begun the first stage of human life; they do not sense much emptiness. One day, when they have earned a degree, obtained a position, and gained material riches, psychological pleasure, fame, and success, they will feel that all is empty, as the Bible says, "Vanity of vanities" (Eccl. 1:2), and "There is nothing new under the sun" (v. 9). These words were spoken by King Solomon, who had a high position and great wisdom. Today as young people you might not have high positions, but all of you at least have graduated from college. This is the time that you feel the need for something. Please remember, what you need the most is not honor and wealth but to gain the Lord Himself. Only by letting Him in can you be a blessed person who lives a blessed human life.

Now we can understand Hebrews 11:24-26. After Moses was born, his mother tried to send him away to prevent him from being killed by the Egyptians. Later, having been adopted by the daughter of Pharaoh, he grew up and received his education in the Egyptian royal palace. But when he had grown up, gradually he came to understand the actual situation, and he no longer wanted to stay in the Egyptian royal palace as the adopted son of the princess. He would rather give up the enjoyment of Egypt and choose God; he considered the reproach of Christ greater riches than the treasures of Egypt. Although in the Old Testament it was not yet the time of Christ, in the eyes of God what Moses did was for Christ. Moses chose Christ and followed Christ.

In the New Testament, we see that the apostle Paul, even though he was a Jew, received a Jewish education and graduated from a Greek university in Tarsus, exhausting all that he could learn of the Greek knowledge, yet like Moses, he forsook everything and chose Christ. Because of Christ he counted everything as refuse. To him, Christ was not only an object of his belief, but Christ was his life, his living, and even the motive, the motivation, and the purpose of his living. Therefore, Christ became his human life, and Christ was his existence. That was why he could say, "For to me, to live is Christ" (Phil. 1:21a).

Each one of us has our own tastes. If someone says, "For to me, to live is an academic degree," "For to me, to live is wealth," "For to me, to live is success and fame," or "For to me, to live is a happy family," he will not be happy; the more he says these things, the more he loses his taste for them. However, the more we say, "For to me, to live is Christ," the more we have the taste. The more we say it, the more we feel blessed and joyful.

THE TESTIMONY OF A BLESSED HUMAN LIFE

From our experience we can truly testify that a blessed human life is a human life with Christ. When we have Christ, we are blessed; when we have Christ, we are joyful. From April of 1925 when I was saved until today, for sixty-two years I have never regretted my believing in Jesus. Although sometimes I do feel that believing in Jesus is quite troublesome, since the Lord says "no" to many things that I feel are all right for me to do, I have never regretted that I believe in Him.

The afternoon I was saved, when I was walking back home, I looked up to the heavens and said, "O God, even if You give me the whole universe, the whole world, I do not want them. I only want You." I made up my mind that even if I had to live on tree roots and drink from mountain brooks, I would preach Jesus for my entire life. In my eyes that was the most joyful thing in the world. However, this vow brought me a lot of troubles. Right after I graduated from school, the Lord came to bother me. He wanted me to serve Him full-time. At that time we did not have the expression *full-time serving one*. There was only the term *preacher,* which refers to a person who carries a Bible bag and goes through every village in the countryside to visit people and talk about Jesus.

I told the Lord that even though I had graduated, my younger brother still had two years before graduation. I needed to work for two years, and when my younger brother graduated, I could then serve Him full-time. The Lord permitted me, so then I had some peace within. Later, my younger brother graduated. At that time the Chinese customs agency was hiring employees, and my brother, because of his proficiency in English, took the test and entered first place to work in customs. His salary was even more than that of a county magistrate. Time passed by, day after day, and one day the Lord Jesus came to me again.

In 1932, seven years after I was saved, a church was raised up in Chefoo where I was. From that time, I started to minister the word in Chefoo. In those seven years, I never stopped pursuing the Lord and reading His Word. Additionally, I met some from the Brethren assembly. The Brethren were the best at expounding the Bible. I attended their meetings and was greatly helped by them. You can say that because in the seven years after I was saved I was working and studying the Bible simultaneously, when the church was raised up, I could immediately minister the word. It got to the point where I gave at least five messages per week. The more I spoke, the more people came. In the spring of the following year, the number of people who were meeting was close to one hundred, and the need became greater and greater. That was when the Lord Jesus came to me again, and He did not let me go this time. He said, "I have prepared everything for you. The church is here, and the work is here." I had no excuse.

In August of 1933 I struggled for nearly three weeks, but inwardly I still was not able to give up my job. I was unsettled within. At that time I reasoned with the Lord again, saying, "O Lord, the saints in the church all have financial difficulties. Most of them can make only about twenty dollars a month. There are about a hundred brothers and sisters. My younger brother makes the most money, and I make the second most. My brother and I provide for many of the supplies used in the meetings, and I also provide for the saints in need. O Lord, if I work, I can help others, but if I do not work, I will need even others to support me."

After three weeks of struggling, one day I asked some responsible brothers and sisters to come together and told them about my situation. That was at a Wednesday night prayer meeting. They all agreed that I should continue to work. It seemed good to them, so I stopped worrying about it. I asked them to pray for me, and they really did pray for me after they returned to their homes. When I went back home at night, I could not fall asleep. I came to the Lord a little after ten o'clock and prayed until about eleven. I clearly felt that the Lord was speaking to me, "This is good enough. We have discussed this matter up to this point. If you still do not believe, then you have rejected Me, the living God, with an evil heart of unbelief." I neither saw the Lord's appearance nor heard His voice, but I actually felt that the Lord was saying to me, "Good enough. This is it! If you would follow Me, then follow. If you would not follow Me, then do not follow. It is you who rejects Me, the living God." I was kneeling down by my bed, so I stood up and told the Lord, "O Lord, I accept; let it be so. Tomorrow I will go to resign from my work. I will quit." At that time, on the one hand I was joyful, but on the other hand I was still quite despondent.

My parents-in-law came to talk with me; they had always respected me. They said, "You have a job that millions of people could not wait to get their hands on, yet you want to quit. How can you do that? Besides, you can work during the day, and in the evening you can still minister the word and serve the church. Would this not be profitable on both ends?" What they said seemed quite logical, but I was very clear within that it was the Lord who wanted me to drop my job, and if I did not follow the Lord in this way, I was finished. Therefore, even though to believe in Jesus is a blessing, sometimes it does not cater to one's desires. In the end, I surrendered; the Lord Jesus won. I resigned from my job the next day.

That morning, before I went to work, I stopped by the post office, because they had notified me of a letter that was addressed to me. That letter was sent from the Presbyterian Church in Changchun, a city in Kirin Province, inviting me to go there to hold a conference for a period of time. I decided then to resign from my job to go and preach Jesus. When I arrived at my company, as I had expected, they would not let me resign. I told them that I would go to Manchuria and hold gospel meetings for three weeks, and that when I came back we would discuss this matter. I went to Manchuria, and the first church there was raised up; twenty or more people, including the elders, preachers, and deacons, all were baptized in the river. While I was rejoicing, my company sent a letter to me, saying that they had decided against my leaving and that, at the end of the year, they would not only raise my salary but also promote me to a better position. Now the temptation came again, for there were only two or three months left before the end of the year when I would receive a bonus. Again, I was troubled within. I thought that maybe I could quit at the end of the year. I made up my mind, thinking that the Lord Jesus should be willing to allow me to stay for two or three months.

After I returned home, my brother told me there was a letter for me. Not waiting to get back to my room, I right away opened the letter in the front courtyard and read it; the letter was from Watchman Nee. Actually, it was not a letter, but only a few short sentences: "Brother Witness, regarding your future, I feel that you should serve the Lord full-time. How do you feel? May the Lord lead you." I was happy yet sad at the same time. I was happy because he wrote the letter during my three weeks of struggling, so I could not deny that it was the Lord's doing, especially since we had not communicated by mail for eight or nine months. He was outside the country at the time, yet he sent this letter right when I was struggling. How could I not be happy? I was sad because if I were to leave my job, would not the bonus for those months go to waste? However, Brother Nee's letter became an encouragement to me, so I left my job. After I resigned, the first thing I did was to go to Shanghai to fellowship with Brother Nee. Brother Nee told me that he was on a ship going from England back to China, and when the ship was going through the Mediterranean Sea, the wind was still and the sea was calm. There he prayed for the Lord's work throughout China. The Lord gave him a feeling that he should write to me, so he wrote that letter.

Therefore, believing in Jesus is a blessing and a joy, but there are also times of struggling. What should we do? In sixty-some years, I have learned the secret of surrendering to Him. The Lord Jesus does not yield; He wants what He wants. If we give it to Him, then we give it to Him; if we do not give it to Him, He will let us do as we will. However, if we give it to Him, we will be blessed; if we do not, sorrow, pain, and remorse will soon follow. Thus, a blessed life is a Christ-life, and a Christ-life is just Christ. Christ will be magnified in our body, whether through life or through death; for to us, to live is Christ (Phil. 1:20-21a). This is a blessed human life, a life of surrender and submission.

(A message given at a young people's conference in Taipei, Taiwan on May 10, 1987)

CHAPTER TWO

KNOWING THE MYSTERY OF THE UNIVERSE AND BUILDING UP THE BODY OF CHRIST

Scripture Reading: Col. 2:2b; Eph. 3:4; John 1:1, 4; 14:9-11, 16-17; 4:24; 6:63; 15:1-5, 16; 21:15-17; Rom. 12:1

OUTLINE

I. The mystery of God—Col. 2:2b.
II. The mystery of Christ—Eph. 3:4.
III. God being life—John 1:1, 4.
IV. God being a person—14:9-11, 16-17.
V. God being Spirit—4:24.
VI. God being the Word—1:1; 6:63.
VII. God needing an organism for the dispensing of life—15:1-5.
VIII. Going forth to bear fruit—v. 16.
IX. Shepherding the Lord's sheep—21:15-17.
X. Preparing to serve full-time—Rom. 12:1.

THE BIBLE OPENING UP THE MYSTERY OF THE UNIVERSE

A gospel booklet entitled *The Mystery of Human Life* tells us that the human life is truly a mystery. The mystery of human life, however, is only a part of the mystery of the universe. There is a mystery in the universe. People who are knowledgeable and reasonable, regardless of their national backgrounds, all share the same feeling and all acknowledge that the universe is difficult and even impossible to explain. Even to this day no one has been able to clearly explain what exactly the universe is, where it came from, and what stories it holds. Why is it that only on the earth there exist human beings, animals, plants, the birds of heaven, the beasts and cattle of the earth, and the fish of the sea? What are the stories behind all these things that exist in the universe? Some say that these things are merely the phenomena of nature, that such changes have been going on for countless ages in the natural world. This kind of explanation at best can give us a little "anesthetic"; it cannot really answer our questions.

In my reading from my youth until now, I have read not only textbooks, the Holy Bible, and Bible-related books; I have also read certain secular books. According to my understanding, while there are many books in the world, there is only one book—the Bible—that is the most complete, clear, and useful in explaining the very truth behind the universe. It may be said that the Bible is neither too much nor too little in its contents, because it has a total of sixty-six books, which were written by more than forty writers over a period of at least one thousand six hundred years. With such a book that was written over such a long period of time by a group of completely different individuals, its contents would naturally be multifaceted. However, whenever I consider this book, the more I meditate on its contents, the more I sense the transparency and clarity of this universe.

Even though in the world there are many scholars, experienced statesmen, and entrepreneurs, they may not have as much understanding concerning the universe as we do. The sphere of their knowledge is limited to what they see with their eyes and what they read from books. Under this situation, they are likely to have a narrow view and also become nearsighted. Therefore, even though they are great statesmen and entrepreneurs, some of them give the impression that they are quite confused. This is because they have an incomplete understanding of the mystery of the whole universe.

KNOWING THE MYSTERY OF THE UNIVERSE IN THE DAYS OF OUR YOUTH

This message is mainly for those who are under twenty years of age. The earlier a person gets to know the mystery of the universe, the earlier he takes hold of the direction for his life. However, if you are over this age, please do not lose heart, because you can be rejuvenated. I truly thank the Lord that He laid hold of me when I was nineteen years old so that I also could lay hold of Him. I regret that I believed so late; if I had been saved a few years earlier, it would have been even better.

Some people wish to marry early, but actually the earlier a person gets married, the more troubles he brings upon himself. All those who marry early are very regretful because the loss they suffer is incalculable. If you want to get married, it is preferable to do it when you are thirty; do not do it when you are twenty-eight, although twenty-eight is still better than twenty-five. Early marriage puts you at a disadvantage. However, you should also not marry too late. To delay until you pass the appropriate age is also not suitable. This is concerning our human experience.

Concerning the knowledge of the universe, since man is the beginning of the mystery of the universe, for a man to wait until he is forty before he knows the mystery of human life is to be too late. I was saved at nineteen, and since then I have grasped every opportunity to love the Lord and know the Lord. Therefore, I hope that all the young people can absorb this message in a good way, because the earlier you get to know the mystery of the universe and the earlier you receive the Lord, the more blessed you are.

THE CHURCH LIFE BEING
A PROPER BALANCE TO HUMAN LIFE

Young people are always seeking for pleasure. They love all kinds of sports and entertainment. Of course, man needs pleasure, and this need is God-created, but such a need has to be kept under control. To illustrate this, we human beings need to eat, and this need was created by God. God created us with a stomach as the organ to digest food, and He also created us with a body to absorb all the nutrition. These are facts. However, God also set various limitations on the amount of food we can take in. We should not overeat, because overeating leads to obesity, and obesity results in illness. There is an old Chinese saying: "Eat one less mouthful at suppertime, and you will live to be ninety-nine." If a person desires to live to an advanced age, he must eat less at dinner-time. If he stuffs his stomach before going to bed, he will kill himself. This is a law for our physical health.

On the one hand, we have to take care of the needs created by God. On the other hand, we should not be excessive, because excessiveness is harmful to our health. Although eating is necessary, overeating is harmful to our physical health. Although entertainment is necessary, too much entertainment is harmful to our mental health. In our human life we need relaxation and proper balance. The more balanced and relaxed we are, the healthier we are naturally. As Christians, we also need entertainment, but our entertainment should not be excessive, and it should be proper. Today in the United States, every kind of entertainment has gone beyond its proper limits; because of this, they have all become corrupted and evil. There are many dark, chaotic, and dishonorable things, and there are numerous cases of people falling into immorality, neglecting their families, ignoring their parents, and disregarding their marriages. All these are due to excessive entertainments. In the United States, you do not even dare to open your eyes in many of the places of entertainment, because all the things going on inside are sinful.

Our meeting life in the church is the most noble and balanced entertainment. We not only have a meeting on the Lord's Day, but we also have meetings during the week. We come together to worship the Lord and to rejoice. This is the healthiest balance to our human life. Therefore, the Christian life is the most balanced and relaxed life. Young people, I advise you that while you are still young you ought to pursue to achieve progress in life, but even more importantly you ought to pursue to know the Lord. By knowing the Lord you will be able to understand the mystery of the universe and the origin of the universe, and consequently you will know how you should live your human life. Therefore, do not consider that going to this meeting or going to that meeting is a waste of time and energy. Our human life needs balance and relaxation, and the church life as a balance can best help us to enjoy a proper human life. The church life really has a proper balancing effect on our human life. If you keep this principle from your youth, you will surely receive the greatest blessing and the maximum benefit throughout your entire life.

THE MYSTERY OF GOD BEING CHRIST

May the Lord give grace to each one of you that, starting at a young age, your eyes would be opened to understand the mystery of the universe. At the very center of the mystery of the universe is God. In other words, the mystery of the universe is God. If God were to be taken away from the universe, there would be no mystery of the universe. That is, if God is taken away, there would be no universe; the universe would not exist. God Himself is the hub, the center, of the universe as a great wheel. If God as the center, as the hub, were taken away, the universe as the wheel would not exist. Therefore, God is the mystery of the universe. The mystery of the universe is God.

Colossians 2:2 tells us that the mystery of God is Christ. This indicates that without Christ, there is no God. The story of God, the mystery of God, is Christ. Christ is God's mystery, God's story. Christ is God. Without Christ, *God* is just a term; with Christ, God becomes a fact, a reality. Where is God? God is in Christ. Who is God? God is Christ. This is why we say that God is not in a mere religion, because without Christ there is no God.

Religion does not have God because it does not have Christ. Likewise, the Chinese Confucianism does not have God because it does not have Christ. Religion talks about moral conduct and cultivation of behavior, and Confucianism talks about human relationships and ethics. Both do not have Christ, so both do not have God. Luke 15 narrates a story of a prodigal son. When the prodigal returned home, he told his father, "I have sinned against heaven and before you" (v. 21). Actually, this translation is not quite accurate. A more accurate translation should be that the son told his father, "Father, I have sinned against you in the presence of heaven." Many expositors of the Bible believe that *heaven* in this story refers to God in heaven. This is similar to the Confucian proverb that says, "There is no one to pray to when heaven is offended." The

Confucian philosophy is pure; it talks about ethics and the relationships among people, and by inference it teaches that in the universe there is a sovereign Being called "heaven." Even though this is quite meaningful, it is without Christ and without God.

The most proper and orthodox religion should be Christianity, which was derived from Judaism. Besides Judaism and Christianity, there is a side branch, which is Mohammed's Islam. The Islam religion was produced by copying the stories from the Old Testament and adding some of the stories of "Isa" in the New Testament. In Mohammedanism Jesus is called Isa because the two names sound similar in the original language. Islam claims that Isa did not die on the cross; instead, when evil men tried to crucify Isa on the cross, a multitude of angels came and rescued him, bringing him up to heaven. Therefore, Isa is greater and higher than Mohammed. Today Isa is in heaven at the right hand of God. It can be said that the Koran is an entire counterfeit of the Holy Bible. In the Koran there are stories about Abraham, Isaac, and Ishmael, but it does not have Christ and God.

The orthodox Christian religion is the only religion that speaks about Christ. Perhaps some would feel that we are self-boasting in that we consider that every other religion does not count, while considering that only the Christian religion counts. Nevertheless, we have to say that whatever counts always counts, and it can never be replaced by any counterfeit. Take gold as an example. Since gold is gold, it cannot be replaced by anything else; neither copper nor any kind of gilding can replace gold, because gold is gold. Likewise, Christ is God, and Christ is simply God; this is the mystery of God.

There is not one religious teacher who would dare to say that he is God. Confucius said, "There is no one to pray to when heaven is offended." He dared not to call himself God, and he never did. Confucius was very humble. Even Islam's Mohammed acknowledged that Isa is the Son of God and is greater than Mohammed. As for Buddhism, it teaches that "a butcher becomes a Buddha the moment he drops his cleaver"; that is, a person can achieve spiritual progress by practicing asceticism. In Buddhism nothing is said about God, and there is no element of God at all.

In all of the religious scriptures, there is only one person who claimed that He is God. Who is this One? He is Jesus Christ (Matt. 26:63-64). Some of the Jews were convinced that He should be condemned and put to death because He told them that He is the Jehovah whom they worship and that He alone is God. The Bible shows us that this person, under the risk of losing His life, told people that He is God. This is quite an amazing thing. Furthermore, no one who adheres to a mere religion says that he is a believer of the Lord. Only those who believe in Jesus are called the believers of the Lord because Jesus is Lord.

THE MYSTERY OF CHRIST BEING THE CHURCH

The mystery of God is Christ (Col. 2:2), and the mystery of Christ is the church. Reading from Ephesians 3:3 through 4 and onward, we can see that the mystery of Christ is the church. Today whoever wants to find Christ must find the church. God dwells in Christ, and Christ dwells in the church; this is the outline of the mystery in the universe. The mystery of the universe lies in God, the mystery of God lies in Christ, and the mystery of Christ lies in the church. However, the so-called church we see today is different from the church mentioned in the Bible. It has deviated and become empty, without reality. In the Bible, the Lord Jesus also spoke in parables concerning this matter (Matt. 13:24-33; 23:25-28). May all the young people clearly see that even though this universe is a mystery, the unraveling of this mystery is with God; this God is in Christ, this God is Christ, and this Christ is in the proper church.

GOD BEING LIFE

Speaking on another aspect, this God who is at the center of the mystery in the universe is life. We know that there are five great religions in the world, yet none of the religious founders dared to tell people that he was God; only Jesus Christ said that He is God. Likewise, not one religious founder would dare to tell others that he was life; only Jesus

Christ said, "I am...the life; he who believes into Me, even if he should die, shall live" (John 11:25).

Of all the philosophies concerning the normal and accepted way of human relationships, the philosophy taught by Confucius of China may be considered the best and the highest. Moreover, the Chinese philosophy can also be considered the most pure and proper philosophy, without any myths and without any strange or absurd ideas. We all know that Greek philosophy contains many myths, Egyptian philosophy contains even more, and Babylonian philosophy has also quite a few. Only the Confucian philosophy of China solely and purely speaks about ethics and relationships between people. Even so, Confucianism never tells people that it is life.

In the history of humankind and in the writings of the Bible, there is only one person who told people again and again that He is life (v. 25). This person is none other than Jesus Christ. The Gospel of John says that Jesus is the Son of God and that He came that we may have life and may have it abundantly (3:16, 10:10). The writings of John are full of descriptions of life, especially concerning eternal life (3:16). This life does not refer to man's mortal life, a created and temporary life; it refers to the eternal life of God. He who believes into the Son has eternal life (v. 36).

Man Being Created in the Image of God

From the Bible, we see the record of God's creation of the heavens and the earth. Genesis 1:1 and 2 says, "In the beginning God created the heavens and the earth. But the earth became waste and emptiness, and darkness was on the surface of the deep." This shows us that God thoroughly cleared up the universe step by step. Then He caused the dry land to emerge from the waters (v. 9) for vegetation to grow. That was the manifestation of the vegetable life (v. 11). Even though plants have life, their life is shallow, and it is a life of the lowest form, a life without consciousness. God then created fish in the waters, birds in the air, and all kinds of beasts on the earth and caused them to multiply (vv. 21-25); so the animal life was brought forth. Though with the animal life there are distinctions of lower and higher forms, it is still not the highest form of life. Therefore, God made man in His image and according to His likeness (v. 26). Thus, the human life came into being.

A group of so-called scholars place the human life and the animal life in the same category. This is a great insult to us. Among them there was one, Darwin, who placed human beings and monkeys in the same class, saying that human beings evolved from monkeys. If such a theory stands, then today on the earth there should be only monkeys and no human beings, or there should be only human beings and no monkeys; but in actuality that is not true. The Bible ranks the human life as the highest created life, because in God's creation of all things He did not create those things in His image and according to His likeness. Only in the creation of man did God make him in His image and according to His likeness (v. 26). Therefore, when we look at a mirror and see our face, we are reminded that we all look like God. Regardless of what people say, there is an unchanging fact—we look like God. We all were made in God's image and according to God's likeness.

The Bible is truly a book of mysteries. It was not until the New Testament time that God became flesh, becoming in the likeness of man (John 1:14). However, in the Old Testament age, one day God brought with Him two angels to visit Abraham (Gen. 18). I believe that those who have read the Bible will remember the story. When Abraham saw three men approaching from far away, he went forth and received these strangers. One of the three was Jehovah. At the time, this Jehovah bore the human image and had a human body, because He had His feet washed and ate the meal Abraham prepared for Him (vv. 4-8). This is God appearing as a man before His incarnation. This is difficult to explain with human language.

In God's creation, the human life is the highest form of life. Suppose we gather some cows, sheep, pigs, dogs, and chicken, and then we ask a man to stand in their midst. Who do you think looks the most beautiful? Certainly the man is the most beautiful. Not only is man the best looking, but he is intelligent and wise. Moreover, man's inward abilities for understanding and judgment are far above all other creatures.

For instance, man's landing on the moon is truly a remarkable accomplishment. Among all of the creatures, what can accomplish such a task? Can a tiger or a lion, or can an eagle or a dove? No, no other animal can accomplish this task except man. The reason that man is the wisest and the most remarkable among all of the creatures is that man was made in God's image and according to God's likeness.

The Transcendent Life Being the Life of God, the Eternal Life

Even though man was made in God's image and according to God's likeness, he still did not have God's life within. This can be likened to molding a human statue; while it has the image of a man, it does not have the life of man. Therefore, Genesis 2 shows us that after God created plants, animals, and man, He placed man in front of the tree of life with the intention that man would receive the tree of life (vv. 8-9). Although the human life is the highest form of life, it is not the transcendent life. The transcendent life is the life of God, the eternal life.

Some who study science define eternity as time plus space. Time plus space is eternity, which is unlimited and boundless. In the universe there is a life that is transcendent and eternal, and that is the life of God. The life of man is high, but it is not transcendent because it is merely a brief, created life. Only the life of God is transcendent, because it is eternal and uncreated. This life is just God Himself.

God's creation in the universe is altogether a matter of life. Take the earth as an example. If there are no plants, animals, or human beings on the earth, the earth would be dead and meaningless. Nobody would want to live on such an earth. Therefore, the creation shows that the universe is a story of life.

Moreover, we know that plants are for the human life and animals are also for the human life. Every plant in the natural world is for man. Some are for man to eat, such as wheat, rice, and various grains; some are for man's admiration, such as the beautiful flowers and pastures; some are for man to utilize, such as tree bark, stems, and leaves. The same can be said of animals. Some are for man to take in as food, such as chicken, duck, and fish; some are for man's employment, such as the horse, donkey, and camel. These are all intended for us. In other words, the heavens are for the earth, the earth is for man, and man is for God.

God Desiring to Enter into Man to Be Man's Life

Since man was made in God's image and according to God's likeness, the life of man is very similar to the life of God. Those with some knowledge of gardening know that grafting requires the two trees to be of a similar kind. Because our life is similar to God's life, the two can be grafted into one; the life of God is able to come into our human life.

When religions talk about God, their emphasis is on signs and works of power. They do not talk about life. Yet in many instances where the Bible talks about God, it speaks about life. To us, God is life; He comes to be our life. Even in Christianity there is a group, the Pentecostals, who mostly focus on how God performs miracles, but they never talk about life. That is a great deviation. In the Bible, God comes to us primarily as life, not as power or signs. The emphasis is on His coming into us to be our life.

GOD BEING A PERSON

In addition, this God is a person. In the so-called religious world, there is a teaching that claims that God is not a person. They believe that God is merely a concept in the human mind, which serves as an object for worship. This kind of speaking concerning God is a great heresy.

The Bible shows us that the God in whom we believe is a person, and as a person He is quite marvelous. Our God is a God who is three yet one. Although God is one, He has three aspects—the Father, the Son, and the Spirit. The Father refers to Himself as "I," and the Son also refers to Himself as "I"; *I* denotes a person. In John 14:10, the Lord says, "I am in the Father and the Father is in Me." In verses 16 and 17, He says, "I will ask the Father, and He will give you another Comforter, that He may be with you forever, even the Spirit of reality." These two passages show us that the Son refers to

Himself as "I"; this Son will ask the Father, and the Father will give us the Spirit. *The Father, I,* and *the Spirit* denote His person. As a person, He has personality. Therefore, our God is not a conceptual object; rather, He is a living person.

Since this God is a person with personality, He has love, mercy, kindness, and even anger; He has the entire range of emotions. Therefore, He is a God as a person, not an abstract object. May you all remember this truth well while you are young. Our God is not something abstract; neither is He a conceptual object of worship. Rather, our God is a person with a personality. Because of this, we human beings are persons, and our person is a reproduction of God. We are persons because God is a person, and we were created according to Him. Therefore, since He is a person, we also are persons. Our God is a God who is a person with a personality.

GOD BEING THE SPIRIT AND THE WORD

Furthermore, this God is Spirit (John 4:24). This is truly wonderful. God is Spirit, and He also created a spirit within us. Today we human beings all have a spirit in us. How marvelous that God is life, God is a person with a personality, and God is also a Spirit. This Spirit is unrestricted; He transcends all physical matters.

Our God is not only Spirit; He is also the Word (1:1). Young people may not know that in this universe there is such a Bible which is the speaking of God. Among human beings, if there were not a Bible, then the entire mankind would fall into darkness, not knowing it is God who created the heavens and the earth, not knowing the stories of the universe, and not knowing the meaning of human life, that is, what a man should be or how a man should behave. But praise God, there is such a book in this world called the Bible, which is the Word of God. When the Lord Jesus was tempted by the devil, the devil asked Him to turn stones into loaves of bread, but the Lord Jesus answered him, "Man shall not live on bread alone, but on every word that proceeds out through the mouth of God" (Matt. 4:4). In the Bible are the words that proceed out of the mouth of God.

The Bible is truly precious. I began my Christian life not

long after the first European war had ended. At that time, Christians in the Western world, especially in Europe, loved to interpret biblical prophecies. Nearly all of the prophecies in the Bible are outlined in the book of Daniel. I was newly saved and began to study the Bible, so all the reference books I bought were of the prophetic nature. As a result, from my youth through more than sixty years, I have read extensively on prophecies in the Old Testament. For example, in Daniel there is a prophecy concerning a ram and a goat fighting against each other (8:3-7). If we read through the entire book of Daniel, we realize that the two animals are symbolic. The ram refers to the Persian Empire, which is today's Iran (v. 20), and the goat refers to the Grecian Empire, particularly during the time of Alexander the Great (v. 21).

Later I studied little by little and gained more understanding. In particular, I read *The Great Prophecies* series written by Brother G. H. Pember, which includes the great prophecies concerning the Jews, the Gentiles, the church, and the entire world. Pember tells us that the prophecies in the Bible are very marvelous. One of the ten great prophecies shows us that Persia is a ram while Greece is a goat, and the two animals fought each other fiercely. History tells us that the bricks in the capital of Persia bore an image of a ram, so that the mark of a ram was everywhere in the city.

Furthermore, after Alexander the Great was crowned, he became the general of the army at only twenty-one years of age. While he was leading the army, he wore horns on his head; the horns he wore were goat horns. Those who have studied Western history might have seen his portrait in their books. Also, the strait between today's Greece and Turkey is called the Aegean Sea. *Aegean* comes from the Greek word for *goat;* even the strait is a "goat strait." This shows us that the Bible is truly the speaking of God.

In addition, we also see from history that Alexander the Great charged through Europe and came to Asia Minor; not long after he landed, he arrived at Palestine, which is the land of Judea. Though many did not welcome him, in the end he won the victory. When he came close to Jerusalem, the Jewish priests showed him the book of Daniel. He understood it, and knowing that the book referred to him as the goat, he was very pleased. For this reason, he treated the Jews favorably. However, in the end, because he was too happy, he ate excessively and eventually met a sudden death. This is what history shows us. In chapter two of Daniel, the prophecy of the great image, revealing the situation from Babylon at the beginning to the "ten toes" at the end, matches perfectly the world situation.

Immediately after I was saved, I started to study the prophecies in the Bible. One of these tells us clearly that the nation of Israel will be restored. At that time I was still quite young and had a strong curiosity. When I read that particular prophecy, on the one hand I was willing to accept it as true; but on the other hand I felt it was something impossible. The nation of Israel had been destroyed for over two thousand years, the land was taken over, and the people were scattered among various nations in the world and assimilated into different cultures. Because of this, the restoration of Israel would not be an easy task. In the eyes of men there was absolutely no chance for it to happen.

In 1948, while working for the Lord in Shanghai, I paid attention to the news every day. One day, the newspaper reported that the Jews had restored their nation. In one incident, the Egyptians came forward to stop them, but a swarm of bees came to aid the Israelis, wounding the Egyptians. I started reading the Bible when I first was saved, and I knew there is a prophecy in the Bible that says God would care for Israel, even sending the hornets to help them (Deut. 7:20; Josh. 24:12). Accordingly, in 1948 the nation of Israel was restored. When I saw the pictures, I realized that the word of God was truly fulfilled.

Although Israel was restored, the old city of Jerusalem was still occupied by the Jordanians, the Arabs. In 1967, nineteen years later, the Israelis recovered Jerusalem. I was ill at the time, but my joy was beyond description. I started reading biblical prophecies during the 1920s, and after more than forty years, the Israelis had recovered Jerusalem. Thus, the prophecy I read was fulfilled; how could I not rejoice (Matt. 24:32; cf. Jer. 24:2, 5, 8; Hosea 9:10)? In the photographs of the recovery of the holy city, I saw the Arabs being chased about by the Israeli army. This is just as the Old Testament had said, that when God comes to save Israel, He will put dread and fear in their enemies (Deut. 11:25). This is quite wonderful. The little nation of Israel is barely noticeable on the world map, yet the many Arab nations that surround her found themselves powerless in dealing with such a tiny piece of land. God's hand was surely in this.

We fellowship about these things simply to illustrate the facts, proving that the words in the Bible are the words of God. Not only are these words prophetic; they are all the more spiritual. Prophetic words are factual, and they are being fulfilled; spiritual words are revelations with the supply of life, and they are also being fulfilled. We know that God is life to us; He is a person, He is the Spirit, and He is the word. When we contact Him, what we touch is the Spirit and the word, and what we receive is life. We touch the Spirit and the word, and we receive life. This life is just God Himself.

GOD NEEDING AN ORGANISM
FOR THE DISPENSING OF LIFE

This God needs an organism. Let us use the human body as an example. Our body is an organism; it is not organized but organic. When we eat, the body digests what we eat. After digestion, the body absorbs and also discharges. Everything that is nutritious to the body is transported to all parts of our body, causing each part to manifest its function. For instance, our ears can hear, and our eyes can see. Even while we are speaking, the ears help to facilitate the organic operations of the body. If our ears were artificial and not able to facilitate the organic operations of the body, we would not be able to hear. If our eyes were artificial and did not have the organic operation, we would not be able to see. In this way, our entire being is an organism.

Since God is eternal life, He needs an organism to express Him as eternal life. In John 15 the Lord says, "I am the vine; you are the branches" (v. 5). The Lord is the vine, and we who believe into Him are the branches. This great vine is an organism for the expression of the life of the vine. Christ with the church is God's organism that operates and works on the earth for the expression of God as the eternal life.

GOING FORTH TO BEAR FRUIT

Today we all are in this organism of Christ. Those who do not understand this organism cannot figure out what we are doing when we come to a meeting. Some of us are seventy- or eighty-year-old seniors, and some are young people in their teens and twenties, but when we come together, we sing and shout, acting as if we are crazy. We do not come together to watch movies or sing popular songs. Rather, when we meet, we simply call on the Lord's name, and we sing and pray. To the unbelievers this is beyond comprehension. However, we are in an organism. When this organism moves, we cannot be still; when this organism goes forward, we cannot hold back. Today when this organism moves and operates, it is for us to go forth and bear fruit. In addition, we do not use the old way but the new way, which is to knock on doors house by house to find the sons of peace.

Formerly we preached the gospel mostly by putting out advertisements, telling people about our gospel meeting and inviting them to come and listen. The result was not very good. We did our best to invite people, making phone calls and even going to the train stations and people's doors, and we prepared love feasts to welcome them. However, not many came. In the past two years, the Lord has given us a new way, to have us go from house to house, bringing the gospel with us. As a result, when we go, God goes, and when God goes, the gospel goes.

When we go door-knocking, we might encounter "packs of wolves," but among them some are sons of peace whom God chose before the foundation of the world. By door-knocking, we seek out the sons of peace. After we have sought them out, it is necessary to fellowship with them. We impart God into them by speaking. John 1:1 says that the Word was God. The words we speak to the sons of peace dispense God into them. The Lord Jesus also said, "The words which I have spoken to you are spirit and are life" (6:63). When we go to speak to the sons of peace, every sentence we speak conveys God, the Spirit, and life. In this way, this organism operates on the earth, and this operation brings forth fruit. Eventually, this great vine bears fruit, filling the whole earth.

I hope that all the young brothers and sisters, after they graduate from college, will go to knock on doors for fruit-bearing. Where should you go? Go to Africa, South America, North America, and Europe; go to all parts of the world and go to all of the nations to knock on doors. How I wish there would be ten thousand young brothers and sisters among us who are trained, each one being able to go out to knock on doors, seeking out the sons of peace. How glorious this would be! After they have completed their education, they do not do anything except one thing, which is to go door-knocking, knocking on all the doors in all corners of the world. After you have finished knocking in South America, go and knock in Central America. After you have finished knocking in Central America, go and knock in North America. After you have finished knocking in North America, go and knock in Europe. Knock in each and every continent. Knock to a point that all across the globe there are young "heroes" from Taiwan knocking on doors.

SHEPHERDING THE LORD'S SHEEP

We like to have the dream that one day there will be five hundred thousand Taiwanese young people knocking on doors all over the earth, and by their door-knocking the Lord Jesus will return. I believe we all have a willing heart, willing to go out and learn door-knocking, seeking out all of the sons of peace so that they can become the Lord's lambs, even in flocks. In the last part of the Gospel of John, the Lord asked Peter, "Do you love Me?" Peter responded, "Yes, Lord, You know that I love You" (21:16). The Lord said to him, "Shepherd My sheep....Feed My sheep" (vv. 16-17).

When we go door-knocking, we find sons of peace and they are saved to become the Lord's sheep who need to be fed by us. How do we feed these new believers? We feed them by having home meetings, establishing many shepherding stations. The result will be not only that Taiwan is gospelized and there is feeding in every home but that this will spread to the whole

world so that the entire earth is doing the same thing. Therefore, our going out for the Lord has a goal with a view. We are
not just passing time; that would be meaningless. We need to
go out door-knocking every day, seeking out the sons of peace
so they may be fruit, be regenerated, and become the Lord's
flock. Then we can set up home meetings to shepherd them
and feed them.

PREPARING TO SERVE FULL-TIME

For the accomplishment of this task, we need preparation,
preparing to serve the Lord full-time. How do we prepare?
Every day we need to contact the Lord, be filled with the
Spirit, and be filled with the Lord's word. We not only know
the Bible and the Spirit, but we are soaked with the Lord's
word and filled with the riches in the Holy Spirit. In this way,
each time we go out to knock on doors, certainly we will be
able to speak forth the Lord.

In the past, some high school students asked what they
should study after graduation. According to the current situation, those who are preparing to knock on doors for the Lord
or to shepherd the flock in the future should study medicine.
If studying medicine is too time-consuming, you can study
languages. There are some languages that you should know. As
Chinese persons, you should study Greek, English, Spanish,
German, and French. If you have the capacity, you can choose
a few more, such as Hebrew. Learning Greek and Hebrew is
for studying the Bible, the Word of God. As for Spanish and
English, these are the most widespread languages in the
world. Additionally, to meet the need in the region of Asia,
some of us need to learn Japanese or Korean.

I hope that one day the young people who go out from
here will preach the gospel either in the Spanish, English,
German, French, Japanese, or Korean speaking world. May
there be young people who are in the organism of the Lord
everywhere, each one door-knocking house by house, seeking
out the sons of peace that they may be saved to be God's flock.
Then the young people can speak the native language and
read the Bible in the native language to feed and shepherd
the native people. This is the new way.

This is a comprehensive fellowship, from the mystery of the universe to door-knocking, fruit-bearing, setting up home meetings, and feeding the Lord's flock. This is for us to apprehend and know the mystery of God so that we can go on to labor in the new way to accomplish the work of the New Testament ministry, which is the building up of the Body of Christ.

(A message given at a young people's conference in Taipei, Taiwan on July 13, 1987)

CHAPTER THREE

HAVING GREAT RESOLUTIONS OF HEART FOR THE LORD

THERE BEING A GOD IN THE UNIVERSE

Dear young friends and brothers and sisters, may the Lord be with you. With a sincere heart, in great rejoicing, and as an elderly person, I would like to speak a few words to you. First of all, it is a sure thing that God exists in the universe. I am over eighty years old, and since my youth I have known God and the Bible. I have studied the Bible in detail with a pure heart for more than sixty years, and the more I read, the more I believe that there is a God in the universe. It can be said that the Bible bears the strongest testimony of God.

If, in the universe, there were not a God who is the sovereign Lord and the almighty Creator, it would not have been possible for the Bible to be written. In the Bible there are not only words of profundity and wisdom but also prophecies concerning the world situation throughout the ages. The more I read these prophecies and observe the world situation, the more I realize that all the events in the world are fulfilling the prophecies in the Bible. Therefore, the Bible makes it impossible for me not to believe that there is a God in the universe.

GOD CREATING MAN THAT MAN MIGHT EXPRESS HIM

The Bible tells us that God created man and moreover that He created man in His image and according to His likeness (Gen. 1:26-27). Hence, man is the most meaningful of all of God's creatures. Man is most meaningful in that God wants man to be like Him and to receive Him. God wants to come into man to be man's life and content so that man might live for Him and express Him on the earth.

THE MEANING AND THE PURPOSE OF HUMAN LIFE

As I see thousands of young people here, I deeply feel that while you are still young and promising, you should see clearly what the purpose of human life is and wherein lies the meaning of human life. You all are studying hard, longing for and striving toward successfully completing your education. For this, I ask the Lord to bless you all that each one of you may be successful in completing your education. However, I would ask you, after you have completed your education, what are you going to do? World culture has already been developed to the utmost. For example, in Taiwan education has raised its standards and has been made widely available. Consequently, you all have been fully enlightened in your understanding. Even though you are quite young, you have already started to consider life. I want to tell you that the meaning of human life lies in God. Without God, man is meaningless; without God, human life is without purpose.

HAVING GREAT RESOLUTIONS IN HEART AND GREAT SEARCHINGS OF HEART— LIVING FOR GOD

The Bible says that among God's people there were great resolutions in heart, and there were also great searchings of heart (Judg. 5:15-16). For whom did they have great resolutions and great searchings? A person of aspiration, though he lives on the earth, always turns his heart to the Lord. We should have great resolutions in heart and great searchings of heart toward God. May all the young people, starting from today, be willing to have great resolutions and great searchings of heart. To have a great resolve is to make a firm decision; to have a great searching is to devise a plan. This is not just to have a resolve but to have a great resolve, and not just to make a plan but to make a great plan. May today be the day that you have a great resolve and make a great plan.

Some may ask, what is the purpose of having a great resolve and a great searching? It is to live for God on the earth.

The meaning of these three words *living for God* is quite broad. In brief, it means to receive God as your life for your entire life. God will lead you to live on the earth for Him. In other words, God will lead you to express Him on this earth by going to every place, every country, and every nation to testify on His behalf and to lead people to know Him.

Due to the advancement of transportation in recent times, the world has become a smaller place. People all over the earth are able to communicate with each other. The world situation today is surely full of darkness and wickedness, and the primary reason is that men do not know God or receive God. If they knew God, they would get out of darkness and enter into light, staying away from wickedness and drawing near to good. Therefore, all of the people on the six continents of the whole globe need to hear the gospel and know the true God so that they could be saved out of darkness into light and out of corruption into the eternal life. Now who will go and do this? Certainly it is you, the younger generation. You should believe in Jesus and receive Him as your life and Savior. Not only so, you should have a great resolve and make a great plan before Him to live for Him.

LEARNING LANGUAGES
TO BEAR WITNESS FOR THE LORD

I would advise you to study hard and endeavor to learn some languages, because one day you all will go to different parts of the world for God to bear witness, to preach the gospel, and to lead people to know God. Today the most common languages are Chinese, English, Spanish, German, French, and Japanese. I hope that as young people you can study hard and endeavor to learn some languages, letting no one despise your youth but being patterns to many. You can choose to learn one or two languages besides your mother tongue.

In addition, I would like to ask the young brothers and sisters to put forth an extra effort in studying Greek. This will be a great help in understanding the Bible. Perhaps in the future some of you will labor to study Hebrew, which is a real necessity in studying the Old Testament. If you are willing to devote and equip yourselves in the study of languages, after you graduate, because of your proficiency in languages, it will be easy for you to find a job in any profession to earn a living so that you can live for the Lord without much difficulty. Even if you go abroad, because you have a few languages as your tools, you will be able to live conveniently while bearing witness for the Lord.

I hope that in the next ten years Taiwan can produce five hundred thousand young people to go all over the world as the Lord's witnesses. I believe that because of your testimony of the Lord in all the tribes and nations in the world, people will be led out of darkness into light. This will not only be for your own honor or for God to be glorified; this will also bring great honor to our nation.

A TESTIMONY

I was born and raised in Christianity and educated in Christianity. Before I was twenty, even though I often went to Christian worship services and also listened to the words of the Bible, I was not saved. I had not had personal contact with the Lord, nor had I personally received Him as my Savior. I did not receive the Lord Jesus until I was nineteen years old. Seven years later, the Lord raised up a church in my hometown through my testimony for Him. From the day I was saved, I had a feeling within me: "Lord Jesus, I want to spend my whole life serving You and bearing witness for You." It can be said that at that moment I had a great resolve and made a great plan to spend my entire life to live for Jesus and to study the Bible.

In the past sixty years, I cannot say that I have had any academic accomplishments, but I can testify that all that I have learned and obtained, as well as my entire heart, are for the Lord Jesus. Initially I had hoped to stay in my hometown, carrying my Bible bag, preaching Jesus village by village, county by county, and city by city, bearing witness for the Lord. However, in His good pleasure He brought me from northern China to southern China, causing me to travel all over on both sides of the Yangtze River. He also brought me from mainland China overseas to Taiwan, and then brought me to Southeast Asia for ten years. Later He brought me again from Taiwan to the United States, and I have been living in the United States for more than twenty years. Today I truly worship the Lord from within my heart, as Judges 5:31 says, "O Jehovah. / ...may those who love Him be like the sun / When it rises in its might."

MAY THOSE WHO LOVE THE LORD BE LIKE THE SUN WHEN IT RISES IN ITS MIGHT

Young brothers and sisters, I hope that from the days of your youth you will have a great resolve and make a great plan to live for the Lord. May you all travel to all parts of the world and to all of the nations, using different languages to bear testimony for the Lord Jesus, glorifying Him so that you may also share in His glory. May your future be, as the Bible says, "Like the sun when it rises in its might." May the Lord bless you according to these words you have heard.

(A message given in the graduation meeting of the young people's training in Taipei, Taiwan on August 2, 1987)

CHAPTER FOUR

THE LORD'S WORK OF RECOVERY IN THIS AGE

THE LORD DESIRING TO HAVE
A GROUP OF PEOPLE WHO LIVE FOR HIM

According to His economy, God created man, accomplished redemption, and produced the church. His desire, however, is that out of those whom He created and redeemed He would gain a group of people who truly live for Him on the earth. Yet two thousand years after God accomplished redemption and produced the church, He has yet to gain this group of people that He longs for.

History shows us that in the Old Testament God had gained the patriarchs throughout the generations and also the people of Israel. Later, the Israelites became degraded. God was greatly disappointed so He judged them. Even today, the Israelites are still under God's judgment. Although God in His grace left them a seed (Rom. 9:29) and also allowed the nation of Israel to be restored in 1948, today in our generation, before our eyes, the nation of Israel is in a condition far away from God, not knowing God at all. What they have passed down through the generations consists only of the Old Testament, which is a book of letters, and Judaism, which is a religion formed with Old Testament laws and regulations. If we travel to the land of Israel, we will see that everything is according to the letter, superstition, ritual, and religion. They know absolutely nothing concerning God, God's economy, and what God wants to gain on this earth. There is a very great gap between what they possess and what we have received in the church in the recent years.

As to the church, in the last two thousand years we can see the Catholic Church, the Protestant churches, and the

Eastern Orthodox Church. Similar to the Jews, they have only the Bible remaining with them. They may read it, but many comprehend only the letter with nearly no understanding of the spiritual significances contained in them and without the knowledge of even the basic truths. In addition, we see a formal religion, that is, the so-called Christianity, which has become a great religion. Even today in Taiwan, there are many pastors and believers in Christianity who are no different from the people in the world. Therefore, even though God created man, accomplished redemption, and produced the church, it seems that He has gained nothing.

GOD'S WORK OF RECOVERY THROUGHOUT THE AGES

Throughout the ages God has been doing a continual work of recovery. He recovers again and again, recovering repeatedly. However, the degradation of the church keeps going downhill. We all know that when a torrent of water rushes down a mountain, nothing can withstand its force. It is impossible to reverse the flow of the water. In one sense, it is truly quite glorious that you and I were born in this age, but in another sense it is painfully sad, because all that we encounter is corruption, degradation, and a downward situation.

Starting from the time World War I ended in 1918, when I was only fourteen or fifteen years old, I paid much attention to the world situation; it has been nearly seventy years since then. When I was studying in junior college, by coincidence, I came across a Chinese newsmagazine. By reading it my eyes were opened, and I started to understand the world situation. While I came to understand historical events from books, I also observed the development of the world situation. I came to the United States in 1961. In 1963, at a meeting where life and truth were released, I spoke a prophecy to all the people there. I said that one day the military forces of the world will gather in the Middle East to fight for the oil fields; because of the oil fields, the world's wealth and its center will shift to the Middle East. This is what I came to understand through sixty years of observation of the world situation and my study of history and biblical prophecies.

We can say that the entire world history is a fulfillment of the prophecies in the Bible. However, the Bible does not have a prophecy concerning a great revival of the church at the end of this age. A century earlier, a group of teachers who expounded the Bible claimed that there would be a great revival. Although I believed their claim at the time, after reading the Bible again, gradually I realized that there is not such a thing. Using the early rain and the late rain in the Old Testament as the basis (Deut. 11:14; Jer. 5:24; Joel 2:23; Zech. 10:1), those teachers said that the early rain denotes the Holy Spirit coming in an early stage, while the late rain denotes the Holy Spirit coming in a later stage, typifying that there will be a revival at the end of this age. They have misinterpreted the Bible. In the Bible, the early rain and the late rain are mentioned not in reference to the church but to the children of Israel.

The last book of the Bible, the book of Revelation written by the apostle John, contains seven epistles. The seven epistles are not long. They point out the errors of the churches, that some commit fornication and others practice idolatry. In principle, almost every epistle tells the church that she should repent and that if she will not, the Lord will come to her in a negative way. Then afterward there is always this word: "To him who overcomes," or "He who overcomes." This shows us that the Bible does not have a prophecy concerning a final revival; rather, it contains promises to the overcomers.

THE LORD'S RECOVERY BEING
TO GAIN A GROUP OF PEOPLE WHO LIVE FOR HIM
ON THE EARTH

Now we would like to see what recovery is. Simply speaking, recovery is to overcome. Therefore, to be in the Lord's recovery is to be in the Lord's overcoming. To be in the Lord's recovery is to turn around, by the Lord's grace, and stand against the tide that is going downhill. This is not to say that we can reverse the tide but that we can stand in the middle of the current and not be carried away by it or flow along with it. This is to be in the recovery. We desire that the churches in the Lord's recovery would all be able to stand against the tide. However, we are displeased and disappointed by the fact that the Lord's recovery has been among us for only a little over sixty years, but in less than a century's time, to our shame there have been some cases of failure every ten years. Some came into the flow of the Lord's recovery, yet after a period of time they failed. Decade after decade, a group of people came in and another group dropped out. Therefore, with great sorrow we say that to this day, even in His recovery, the Lord has not been able to gain the group of people He wants to gain.

For this reason we have initiated the practice of changing the system and taking the new way. By *changing the system* and *taking the new way* we mean that we drop the old things and begin anew with a new way. What is the new way? It is the way that fully meets the Lord's standard. What the Lord desires today is to gain a group of people that fully meets His standard, living on the earth for Him.

In Genesis the first matter mentioned after God created man was related to eating. "Behold, I have given you every herb yielding seed that is on the surface of all the earth and every tree which has fruit yielding seed; it shall be for you as food" (1:29). Food is of supreme importance to the Chinese, and it is even more so to God. In the past in China, when we went out to invite people to hear our gospel preaching, we were frequently asked by some naughty ones, "Does Jesus provide meals? If He does, I will definitely go." Of course, Jesus provides our meals; in God's ordination man needs to eat for his existence.

The second matter mentioned in the Bible is marriage (2:18-25). Eating is for man's existence, while marriage is for man's continuation. The Bible does not say that eating should be held in high regard, but it says, "Let marriage be held in honor among all" (Heb. 13:4). The third matter mentioned in the Bible is clothing. God made for man coats of skins to cover his body (Gen. 3:21). The traditional but incorrect concept is that when we begin to love the Lord, we do not care about eating, marriage, and clothing. In other words, we give up everything and care only for the Lord. In actuality, eating, marriage, and clothing are three great necessities of human life. We are not to give them up, but we should not be occupied with them. We do not live for eating, marriage, or clothing; we live for the Lord. Today, however, two thousand years after Jesus accomplished redemption, God still has not gained such a group of people.

THE SIGN OF THE LORD'S SECOND COMING

According to our study of biblical prophecies and the world situation, we truly feel that today we are in the last age. God will speed up His move in this last age. The nation of Israel has been restored, which is a fulfillment of a great prophecy in the Bible. Israel was taken captive in 606 B.C., yet after twenty-five centuries it stands again as a nation. Israel lost the land and was carried away to the nations. The Jews lost their nationality and were naturalized in different countries, becoming immigrants in the nations. It is incredible that for such a group of people their nation could be restored after twenty-five centuries.

In 1948 in Shanghai, my heart leapt when I saw the headline on the newspaper: "The Nation of Israel Restored." I had studied this prophecy since 1925, and after twenty-three years I witnessed the fulfillment of this great prophecy in the Bible—the restoration of the nation of Israel. What a miraculous event! Jerusalem, the capital of the Jews, was trampled by the Gentiles, but the Bible says clearly that in the last days Jerusalem would be returned to Israel. In 606 B.C. King Nebuchadnezzar trampled Jerusalem and desecrated its temple. Eventually he brought the vessels of gold and silver, which were used in the worship of God, and put them in the temple of his gods. Babylon is the present Iraq, and Iran is Persia in the Bible; the present war between Iran and Iraq is a war between Persia and Babylon.

In June of 1967, nineteen years after the restoration of the nation of Israel, one day, which was the last day of the Six-Day War, Jerusalem was returned to Israel; it was retaken by the Israelis. Prior to that time Jerusalem was in Jordan's possession. I can never forget that day. I was in the hospital for a surgery, lying on my hospital bed, but when I saw the news of Jerusalem being returned to Israel, I almost jumped out of bed. I truly wanted to sing hallelujah! Nineteen years before, in Shanghai I saw the headline "The Nation of Israel Restored" in the newspaper; nineteen years later, in a hospital bed in America, I heard the news that Jerusalem was returned. From that day on, surrounding the small nation of Israel there have been more than twenty Arab, Islamic nations whose armies exceed the total population of Israel. These nations have been watching Israel like a tiger eyeing its prey. However, they have had no way to defeat Israel. Who is doing this?

We know that the sign of the Lord's second coming is the consummation of this age. Matthew 21:19 and 20 says that the Lord Jesus became hungry, and seeing a fig tree on the way but not finding any fruit on it, He cursed the tree so that it would no longer bear fruit, and it instantly dried up. The fig tree is a symbol of the nation of Israel. When the Lord came to the children of Israel, He could not find any fruit among them; consequently, they came under His curse. Therefore, after the Lord ascended, the nation of Israel began to suffer many hardships.

According to the Jewish historian Josephus, Jerusalem was completely destroyed by the Roman armies under the Roman prince Titus in A.D. 70. The Lord prophesied in Matthew 24 that the temple would by no means be left a stone upon a stone which would not be thrown down (v. 2). From that day, the Jews have not been having an easy time in the world. They lost their citizenship, wandering on the earth and being persecuted by others. The greatest atrocity occurred during the Second World War when Hitler gathered millions of Jews from within countries under German occupation and executed them in gas chambers. This caused the Jews all over the world to be united. Since they realized that even if they became German citizens, Germany would not protect them, they knew they must be united. These things are laid out before our eyes, which cause us to realize that today we are in the end times. In Matthew 24 the Lord says that when you see the branch of the fig tree becoming tender and putting forth its leaves, you know that the summer is near (v. 32). The summer is the day of the Lord's coming, and the branch's becoming tender and putting forth its leaves is the restoration of the nation of Israel, which will be the time of the Lord's second coming.

THE LORD'S RECOVERY IN THIS AGE

In such a time the Lord must take the quick way. He must quickly gain a group of people whom He has not gained before to be His overcomers on this earth and His bride to welcome His return. These days, in a formal wedding the bridegroom always arrives first, and the bride enters a few minutes later. It is considered inappropriate for the bride to arrive earlier than the bridegroom. In the wedding in the New Testament, however, instead of the Bridegroom waiting for the bride, the bride is waiting for the Bridegroom. In the parable in Matthew 25 it is the ten virgins who take their lamps to go forth to meet the bridegroom (v. 1), but who is going forth to meet the Bridegroom today? We have yet to meet a group of Christians who are going out of the world to meet Christ, the Bridegroom. Instead, most Christians are in the world. Today the Lord wants to gain a group of people who take their lamps and go forth to meet Him, the Bridegroom. May we be that group of people.

Today even the pastors and preachers may not realize that we need to become the group of people whom the Lord desires. If you go and ask a pastor, "Is there a statement in the Bible concerning virgins going forth to meet the bridegroom?" He may answer, "Is there such a statement? I just know that we have to love our parents, we have to love others as ourselves, the husbands have to love their wives, the wives have to submit to their husbands, and we have to be humble and patient." This is the condition of Christianity today. Therefore, regardless of what we are busy with in our daily living, we should not forget that the most important thing is to properly adorn ourselves and be prepared to go forth to meet our Bridegroom. We need to be the group of people who is preparing to meet our Bridegroom. We all need to go forth, to go out from this world, to meet our Bridegroom.

How do we prepare to meet our Bridegroom? Matthew 24 says, "But learn the parable from the fig tree: As soon as its branch has become tender and puts forth its leaves, you know that the summer is near" (v. 32). In the same chapter it also says, "And this gospel of the kingdom will be preached in the whole inhabited earth for a testimony to all the nations, and then the end will come" (v. 14). On the one hand, the end, the summer, is near, which is this age; but on the other hand, the gospel has yet to be preached in the whole inhabited earth. Some Christian fanatics have said, "The Lord Jesus is coming tomorrow." According to both sides of the prophecy in the Bible, that is still not possible. Back in 1936, I was working in Tientsin. At that time there was a brother named Panton in England who was gifted in interpreting prophecies. Many who pursued the Lord read his biblical interpretations and prophecies. However, Panton made a big mistake. He displayed two pictures. One picture was that of Nero, whom Panton claimed would become Antichrist; this was also the Caesar Nero who killed Paul. The other picture was that of the Italian prime minister Mussolini, whom Panton speculated to be the coming Antichrist. I very much admire Mr. Panton's biblical interpretations, but for some reason he made this big mistake. At that time the Antichrist could not have appeared, because spiritually the preparation of the gospel was still inadequate.

Fifty-one years afterward, which is half a century later, the gospel still has not been preached in the whole inhabited earth. The gospel has not been fully spread even in the little island of Taiwan. Whose responsibility is this? Do you believe the gospel can be fully spread in Taiwan by those who are in Christianity? Can we do it according to our old way? We practiced the old way for over thirty years. In the first ten years we were quite successful, but in the last twenty years we have been a complete failure. Therefore, we have initiated a change, changing back to the biblical way. The preaching of the gospel to the whole inhabited earth began from Jerusalem. To us, Taiwan is our "Jerusalem," so we need to preach the gospel here in Taiwan.

Based on my observation, I have a deep feeling. Since the dawn of history there has never been a mission, an evangelical group, a Christian organization, or a great evangelist that did not want the door of the gospel to be opened to them; yet none of them has had their desire fulfilled. William Carey went to India, David Livingstone went to Africa, and Hudson Taylor went to inland China, but the gospel was not spread to the whole earth through them. However, today the whole world is opened to the Lord's recovery. This is not an exaggeration. If we have one thousand brothers and sisters, each one can immediately be sent out, because Western Europe is opened, New Zealand is opened, Australia is opened, and even Eastern Europe, Africa, South America, and Central America are all opened up. Every letter sent to us from the major continents all over the globe has fellowshipped with us regarding the need for people to go. But where are the people? We do not have enough people even to meet the need of Taiwan, or even just Taipei, not to mention the whole earth. Where are the people?

THE REASON FOR THE WHOLE EARTH'S BEING OPENED TO THE LORD'S RECOVERY

Why is it that every place in the world is opened to the Lord's recovery? First, it is because we are standing on the proper ground. In order to wage a war, we need to have a just cause. Certainly we have a cause—we boldly proclaim the unique ground of the church everywhere we go. When we proclaim this, the moment we sound the trumpet, we prosper wherever we go. The reason Christianity does not like us, the Lord's recovery, is that we keep the unique ground of the church. Roughly thirty or forty years ago, some Western missionaries commented about us, saying that everything about the "Little Flock" is good and that the only bad thing is the teaching concerning one church for one city. However, the Bible clearly reveals that universally the church is one, and practically it is one church in one city. Today those who truly pursue the Lord are willing to open to this recovery because this recovery is waging a war with a cause.

The second reason is that the truth is among us. Today Hong Kong is the hub of the Chinese-speaking Christian meetings in the Far East, and all sorts of Christian publications can be found there. However, how much truth and how much spiritual value can we see in those publications? This is not only the situation in the Chinese-speaking world in the Far East but also the situation in the English-speaking world in the West. However, in the Lord's recovery, the truth pours out as a waterfall. This is why a particular book on reading the Bible, published by a certain seminary, points out that the exposition of the Bible by Christians in the Chinese-speaking world over the past forty years has not been able to escape the influence of "the local church."

Take South America for example. The whole of South America is open to the Lord's recovery because in the recovery there is the church ground and the biblical truth. In addition, the saints in Africa say that they can conquer the whole continent with just the New Testament Recovery Version, the life-studies, the *Life Lessons,* and the *Truth Lessons;* the saints in South America, Central America, New Zealand, and Australia also say the same thing. While the Lord has not yet gained what He wants to gain, throughout the generations, even in this last age, the Lord has in fact raised up a group of people on the earth who love Him and love the truth.

In the twentieth century, in an age where transportation, printing, television, and all kinds of communication devices are convenient, the books and periodicals we have published have been spread to all the continents. The Lord's recovery does not merely belong to us who are only a small number, but the Lord's recovery belongs to all of God's children. People are open to the Lord's recovery because here we have the proper church ground and the biblical truths. We have both of these here today, so the Lord's recovery has a way.

THE GOAL OF HUMAN LIFE

The top human life is a life that takes this way of the Lord. This way matches the purpose of God's creation of man and also meets the requirements of the revelations in the Bible. What kind of life can satisfy us? Is it a life that makes a lot of money? Is it a life that obtains a high position? What is the most valuable thing in our life? To put it bluntly, nothing is valuable. Human life in the world is no more than merely a matter of food, clothing, and marriage. How valuable are these things? A person studies, labors, and strives in order to receive a high education, obtain a good job, and have a good future; yet in the end when he dies, he has nothing.

We are on this earth not without a goal. We are not here merely to take in food, to put on clothes, and to get married. Rather, we have a positive goal. Suppose we take the way of the world to become a prominent scholar or even a president of a university. What then? Every one of us will die and be buried, and when that day comes, we cannot take anything with us, not even one dollar or one diploma. However, if we take the way of the Lord, even if the Lord delays His return and we "fall asleep," when we meet the Lord we will have boldness because we are not empty-handed; we bring with us those whom we have led to salvation.

Imagine if the Lord delays His coming for twenty or thirty years, and the young people of this generation go forth with a burden to Africa, South America, Australia, and New Zealand, leading multitudes of people to salvation. How glorious this will be! They will go not to earn dollars, marks, or francs; instead, they will gain Americans, Germans, and French. How valuable and meaningful that would be! Do not worry about what they will eat. There will be no problem. The Lord Jesus provides our meals, and the meals He provides are sweeter and richer than those provided by men. Therefore, we have to burn the campuses and communities with the fire of the gospel, bringing people into the Lord, the value of which will last for eternity.

PREPARING OURSELVES IN SEVERAL MATTERS

Now we need to prepare ourselves in several matters. First, we must pursue and grow in the spiritual life, earnestly maintaining a living fellowship with the Lord, fully consecrating ourselves to Him and having proper dealings before Him. We are contacting not merely a religious object but a living person. He is the living Spirit who dwells in our spirit. Therefore, we can fellowship with Him and receive His shining, guidance, and supply, allowing Him to regulate us in great or small matters so that we may have genuine growth in life.

Second, we must be equipped in the truth. People read the

Bible in black and white according to their own understanding, barely scratching the surface. In particular, the Chinese are filled in their mind with things such as filial piety, honor, humility, patience, and forgiveness. For this reason, when they read the passages in the Bible that talk about honoring the parents, loving the wives, and submitting to the husbands, they feel that these things are very good, because they are similar to the virtues taught by the ancient Chinese sages. Actually, the Bible is full of the light of truth and the revelation of Christ. We need to read and get the word into us, and we also need to read and get ourselves into the word so that we may be mingled with the word.

The Recovery Version of the New Testament can be called the crystallization of the understanding of the divine revelation, which the saints everywhere have attained to in the past two thousand years. Therefore, now we can simply open the Recovery Version, and regardless of which book, chapter, verse, or sentence we read, there are some footnotes and explanations that enable us to fully understand it at a glance and immediately see clearly as the veils in heaven open before us. We need to labor on these revelations and this light by studying and pray-reading them again and again, thereby equipping ourselves with the truth.

Third, we need to build up a good character. We have to admit that although we have a God-created character in us, our fallen and corrupted character is loose, lazy, careless, and sloppy. In 1953 when I held a training in Taipei, I put together a small book on thirty character traits—being genuine, exact, strict, diligent, broad, fine, and others—hoping that we could exercise to cultivate them little by little. We should not merely read them and quickly forget about them, like the Chinese who read the books written by Confucius and Mencius. We need to exercise ourselves in these thirty items to build up a character that is useful to the Lord. We need to pray to the Lord, because although we do not have the strength to do this, the Lord is the bountiful supply within us. In Philippians 4 Paul says, "What things are true, what things are dignified, what things are righteous, what things are pure, what things are lovely, what things are well spoken of...take account of these things" (v. 8).

These things are all related to character. Then Paul goes on to say, "I am able to do all things in Him who empowers me" (v. 13). Therefore, we can all build up a good character in Him who empowers us.

Fourth, we must receive a higher education. In the process of receiving our education we should learn some languages, especially English, the international language with which we must become proficient. In addition, we should learn at least one other foreign language, be it Spanish, German, French, Japanese, or Korean. These are all major languages that are commonly used in the world today. In brief, we need to be familiarized with two other languages besides Chinese. Not only so, we also need to study and get into the depths of the Bible. For this purpose, it is best that we learn some Greek. The more we learn of literature and languages, the better it is. We must attain to some depth in the study of languages.

Fifth, we need to know history, recognize the situation and the tide of the world, and be aware of the condition on the earth today. We need to pay attention to these five items: life, truth, character, language, and common knowledge. We need to endeavor to practice these things while paying attention to our living. The Lord is living; to be sure, He can bear all of our responsibility. Moreover, today the Lord's recovery on the earth is widespread. In this widespread recovery, we mutually care for and supply the needs of each other, which is a great help. Therefore, you should not be anxious; rather, you should diligently equip yourselves by laboring on these matters—life, truth, character, language, and a knowledge concerning world culture, history, current events, and present trends. In this way, we will be able to advance toward the goal to gospelize Taiwan, Japan, Europe, Australia, and New Zealand. May the Lord bless us with His presence.

Through the years I have truly seen the sovereignty of the Lord's hand over everything. In 1971 when I went to Australia and New Zealand, they did not welcome Chinese people. Today within sixteen years, the doors of these two countries are opened wide to the Chinese. Therefore, the Chinese have gone to these countries in flocks. That is the Lord's preparation for us. If we go there now, we will see the Chinese everywhere;

that is very convenient for us. Likewise, if we go to the United States now, whether we go to Los Angeles, New York, or Chicago, it is no different than being in Taiwan. We are able to buy in these places everything that is available in Taiwan.

If Taiwan is to produce five hundred thousand brothers and sisters for the spread of the gospel overseas, then we need to have five million saints in Taiwan so that one out of every ten saints can go out. The people from Taiwan gospelizing the entire world, and the brothers and sisters from Taiwan trekking all over the earth—what a wonderful prospect that would be! Where will you go—to Africa, South America, Central America, North America, Eastern Europe, or Western Europe? We can pray to the Lord, "O Lord, where should I go? O Lord, where do You want me to go?" May we all answer the Lord, "O Lord, here am I; send me."

(A message given at a college conference in Taipei, Taiwan on August 6, 1987)

CHAPTER FIVE

THE SPREAD OF THE LORD'S RECOVERY

We all hope that our human life is a blessed human life, and we all wish to enjoy blessing and happiness. The Chinese pay much attention to being blessed with good fortune and happiness. For a person to have a blessed human life, he must first obtain the source of blessing. The real source of blessing is none other than God Himself. The Lord Jesus is the embodiment of God, and He is also the expression of God. He is the practical source of blessing in human life. When we have the Lord Jesus, we have the source of blessing, and when we have the source of blessing, we have a blessed living. The source is like a fountain, and the living is like a flow. The Lord Jesus lives in us as our source, and we live out the Lord as His course, His flow. As to how the Lord flows out of us, that is a matter of outlet. Even with a riverhead and a watercourse, without an opening this river cannot flow freely. For instance, the Yangtze River runs through the whole of China and eventually finds an outlet and flows into the East China Sea. The Lord who lives inside of us also wants to flow out of us. Therefore, we are now faced with the matter of outlet.

THE RECOVERY AMONG US BEING
A RECOVERY OF THE TRUTH

Before the early apostles passed away, the vision of God had been completely revealed, but on the other hand, the church had also become degraded and gone downhill. We can see traces of the degradation of the church in 2 Timothy, 2 Peter, 2 John, and 3 John. The church's degraded condition on earth worsened step by step. However, regardless of how

Satan causes the church to become degraded, God's hand that holds the church has never let loose. Because every word in the Bible shall by no means be annulled but shall be fulfilled, God's hand has always been rescuing. This rescuing is the recovery.

We know from history that the church went through a long period of great darkness, and this dark age lasted for ten centuries, from approximately A.D. 500 all the way up to A.D. 1500, from the gradual formation of the Catholic Church to the Reformation beginning with Luther. During this period, the Bible was a closed book to man. It was not until after the Reformation that the Lord raised up some to open up the truths in the Bible.

In the 1700s, the Lord raised up N. L. von Zinzendorf in Moravia, and the biblical truths shone brightly. After 1820, the Lord again raised up a group of His lovers who were called "the brothers." Later, people called them the Brethren. Among them was Brother J. N. Darby, who gave a very thorough exposition of the Bible. In church history he is known as the "king of Bible exposition." The Brethren not only had the light in their biblical exposition, but they were also strong in their spirit. However, their biblical exposition gradually tended toward letters and thus annulled life, so that eventually all that remained were empty letters in black and white. Furthermore, due to the differences in the interpretation of truth among themselves, the Brethren also underwent division after division, so that in the end they completely lost their influence.

In *The Orthodoxy of the Church*, Watchman Nee says that the church in Philadelphia refers to the Brethren assembly at its most flourishing time. However, the Brethren declined and became Laodicea. In the early twentieth century, Europe and America, the two most influential continents in the world, were utterly damaged by Christianity. They were like fields planted in a messy and cluttered way without any room to plant something else. Therefore, God chose China, sowing the seeds of recovery in that virgin soil. This is the beginning of the recovery among us.

From 1922, when our first meeting was raised up in

Foochow, until now, it has been exactly sixty-four years. The Lord's greatest recovery among us is not in power, nor is it merely in the matter of life or the church. The Lord's most prevailing recovery among us is the recovery of truth.

Brother Nee was only in his thirties when he first attended the Keswick Convention. When he opened his mouth to speak, people were immediately subdued by the clear truths he presented. It was the same way when I went to the United States twenty-eight years ago. The truths I spoke astounded the pastors and preachers in the audience. They had never heard such clear truths.

In the United States I traveled back and forth between the east and west coasts for over ten years, visiting place after place, and afterward churches were raised up in those places. In 1974, the Lord gave me the burden to release the life and light in the New Testament and the understanding of the Word. Therefore, I no longer traveled frequently. Instead, I spent six months every year to write outlines and footnotes in preparation for the ten-day trainings in summer and winter. Over eleven years we have had twenty-two trainings, covering the Gospel of Matthew, the first book of the New Testament, to Revelation, the last book.

The Lord truly did an extraordinary work among us. The release of the truth has been a strong revival in the history of the church, which the Lord has given to us. We expound the Scriptures neither according to theology nor according to tradition. Rather, our way of expounding the Word is according to the experience of life. Our understanding of the Bible comes from our personal experience of life and our observation in leading the churches. In more than ten years of releasing the truth, the Lord granted us much precious light from the first book of the New Testament to the last book.

THE LORD'S RECOVERY SPREADING
TO THE WHOLE EARTH

Through the recovery of the truth, the Lord raised up many churches in all parts of the world. In 1949 in the Lord's recovery there were less than a hundred churches overseas, most of them being in Southeast Asia, including the Philippines,

Thailand, Indonesia, and Malaysia. But from 1949 to 1984, not counting mainland China, there were more than six hundred churches in the six major continents. Today there are more than one hundred churches throughout North America, in the United States and Canada. Central America plus South America also have more than a hundred churches. Thus, there are a total of more than two hundred churches in the Americas. In addition, Europe, Africa, and Australia have about eighty or ninety churches, plus more than a hundred in the Philippines, over twenty churches in Japan, and over twenty churches in South Korea. There are more than six hundred churches altogether in the East and the West, scattered throughout the six major continents of the world. Recently the Lord's work has come even to India and Burma. This shows us that the churches in the Lord's recovery are everywhere in the six major continents over the whole globe.

Through us the Lord first recovered the truth. Next, through the recovery of the truth He spread His testimony to every place. This spread was not only in one continent or several countries but in all six major continents. Fifty years ago in a conversation between Brother Nee and me, we both saw this matter very clearly. Although we were raised up by the Lord in China, the Lord's recovery was not merely for the Chinese people but for the whole world. Back then we did not know how the Lord's recovery would spread out, because we were born in China and grew up in China, and the vast land of China was more than enough for us to do the Lord's work.

In 1949 before we left Shanghai, there were more than four hundred churches, with co-workers in thirty-three provinces. Shanghai was the biggest church and the center of the work. At that time I was serving in Shanghai while Brother Nee was focusing on conducting the training on Mount Kuling. That was truly a wonderful scene. However, the political situation changed suddenly, so Brother Nee sent me to Taiwan. At that time my view reached only as far as Japan and Southeast Asia. Unexpectedly, the Lord led me to live permanently in the United States in 1962, thereby bringing the truth of the Lord's recovery to the English-speaking world.

After World War II, having become the leading nation in

the world, the United States spread its influence throughout the entire earth. As a result, after the Lord's recovery came into the United States, within ten years it spread to the Americas, Europe, and Australia. It was the Lord who accomplished all these things. Today Central and South America are completely open to the Lord's recovery. Even if we send up to a thousand full-time workers, still they would not be enough to meet the need of these places.

While observing the world situation in 1984, I saw that under the Lord's sovereignty the island of Taiwan has a wealth of talents, a high level of education, a thriving economy, and a low crime rate. Then I thought of preparing one thousand full-timers who would first receive the training and then go marching into the villages and small towns to "gospelize," "truthize," and "churchize" Taiwan to make it a model for the spread of the Lord's recovery. At that time you all declared fervently, "O never speak of sacrifice! / A privilege untold / Is to be His at any price, / In Calv'ry's hosts enrolled" (*Hymns,* #473, stanza 2). I was greatly touched. We used one thousand full-timers as the base number in our preparation to gospelize Taiwan. We planned to first gospelize Taiwan and then bring the truths of the Lord that had been recovered among us to every corner of the world.

The raising up of the churches in Australia, Europe, Africa, and America is mainly through the literature in the Lord's recovery. However, the literature alone is not adequate; there is the need for people to go and strengthen them. South America, Europe, and Australia have always hoped for people to go to help them. It is well known that the best place for producing workers is Taiwan. The current phase is to have all the full-timers go through a year of training in Taiwan, work through every town and village in Taiwan, and then set out to go overseas. In the soon-to-be-launched Full-Time Training, those who join the training must first study Greek and learn its grammar; then they will be able to use reference books and dictionaries. Second, they must learn English so that they can at least read and speak it. Third, they need to choose and learn either Japanese or Spanish. In this way, the needs of various places can be met.

After a year of training, the trainees will be sent out to every city, town, and village to preach the gospel and to stay to lay a solid foundation for the church there. During this period, they should come back every few months to continue to study foreign languages until they can listen, speak, and write. After learning for a few years, the trainees should have a solid foundation of the truth with much practical experience in how to preach the gospel, how to lead others, and how to build up the church. Then regardless of where they are sent, they will be able to considerably strengthen the church in that locality.

Taiwan is the training base, as well as the nursery, of the Lord's recovery. From here we will begin to bring the truth to every continent in the world step by step.

THE LORD'S RECOVERY SPREADING OUT FROM TAIWAN

Today my greatest joy is that the Lord is the source of my blessing, the flow of my blessing, and even more, the outlet of my blessing. In faith I can see one thousand trained full-timers springing up from the small island of Taiwan to saturate the entire island, including the mountainous regions, with the gospel and truth. This will cause the whole earth to see that within the six continents there is a little island that has churches not merely in the big cities but even in all the villages. Furthermore, the world will see that the gospel these people preach is a high gospel, the truth they have is transparent, and their understanding of the Bible is thoroughly clear.

In the next few years, in step with the promotion of the truth, the Recovery Version of the New Testament in English, Chinese, Japanese, Korean, German, French, Portuguese, and Spanish will be completed one after another. This will be the best means by which we can go out and proclaim the truth. Equipped with such a Recovery Version, all those who have gone through the Full-Time Training and who have learned the truth, preached the gospel in the communities, built up churches in villages, and gained proficiency in several foreign languages will go to all parts of the world. At that time those who are preaching the gospel, speaking the truth, and building up the churches in all parts of the world will all be from Taiwan. The thought of such a long term vision brings me much joy. I believe that this vision will be fulfilled in time, and its fulfillment will not be too long from now. May none of us be slack, but rather pray much for the Lord's spread in Taiwan.

We all know that after Mary conceived and gave birth to Jesus, Zachariah (Luke 1:67-79), Elizabeth (vv. 41-45), Simeon (2:28-32), and Anna (vv. 36-38) all spoke prophecies, and Mary "kept all these things and pondered them in her heart" (v. 19; cf. v. 51). *Kept...in her heart* in Greek means to carefully keep and remember in her heart. Mary carefully kept and remembered these prophecies in her heart. Then one day she saw with her own eyes the fulfillment of each of these prophecies. I hope you would also carefully keep and remember these words. What we speak is not something idealistic nor something in a dream. What we speak is a specific way. One day you all will see the fulfillment of these words.

Lastly, I hope that those who go out for the propagation of the Lord's recovery will not merely have a clear understanding of truth but will also be properly dressed. This shows others that the people of the kingdom of the heavens are a noble group of people. Regardless of whether we are in a large meeting or a home meeting, everyone should be properly dressed with appropriate attire. This should be the outstanding feature of our living on the earth, since we are people with a heavenly calling. I hope that not only the trainees will practice this but that all the saints in the churches will also do the same thing. Regardless of the kind of meeting it is, everyone should dress appropriately.

Above is our overall plan, and we are now pressing forward toward this goal. Our goal is not merely to gospelize, truthize, and churchize Taiwan but even to use Taiwan as a model and a starting point to gospelize, truthize, and churchize the entire world.

God promised Abraham, saying, "In your seed shall all the families of the earth be blessed" (Acts 3:25). Today this promise has yet to be fulfilled. Now we have inherited this promise that in us all of the people in Taiwan and in the whole world will be blessed. We are delivering the gospel not only to the whole island of Taiwan but also to the whole world so that all of the people may receive the Lord Jesus as the source of blessing in their human life.

(A message given at the graduating college seniors conference in Taipei, Taiwan on June 1, 1986)

CHAPTER SIX

THE BROAD HIGHWAY
OF THE LORD'S RECOVERY

Scripture Reading: 1 Thes. 1:9-10; 2:19-20; 5:23-24; Matt. 24:14;
Acts 1:8-11; 2 Tim. 4:7-8; Rev. 22:17, 20; 14:1, 4b

GOD REVEALING VISIONS TO MAN THROUGH DREAMS

In the Bible, dreams are very close to the visions given to
man by God. The dream Jacob had became his vision (Gen.
28:10-17), and the dream Joseph had also became his vision
(37:5-11). In the Bible there are many others who saw visions
in their dreams.

I was saved in April of 1925, and from then on I loved the
Lord and desired earnestly to know the Bible. At that time I
was young and strong, and both my thoughts and intellect
were still developing. However, the Lord laid hold of me, and
He caused me to spend willingly the most precious years of
my life entirely on Him and His Word. Thus, from the reading
of the Word I saw the significance of dreams and visions.

Since everyone has dreams, it seems that dreams should
be meaningless. Nevertheless, the Bible uses dreams to reveal
to us the visions of God. The Chinese Bible uses the expression *strange dream*. A strange dream is a dream in which
a person sees some uncommon scenes; hence, it is called a
strange dream. The English word *vision* denotes a scene, just
as a television broadcasts numerous different scenes.

Now I would like to tell you about an extraordinary dream
I had in 1943. What God showed me in that dream was not
a common scene. Rather, what He showed me was a vision, a
strange and miraculous scene. Although I had known the Bible
since my youth, before 1943 I had never had any uncommon

vision or scene in a dream in my twenty years of being a Christian.

In the evening of July 7, 1937, the night of the Marco Polo Bridge Incident, I was on a boat from Chefoo on the way to Tientsin; the next morning I disembarked at Takukou, which was the biggest port in the north. That morning it was unusually quiet; not a soul was to be found. I continued by train, and when it arrived at the Tientsin station, there was a child selling newspaper extras. I read the extra and found out that on the previous night Japan had instigated the Marco Polo Bridge Incident and had begun its invasion of China. Because of this, there were wartime conflicts from Tientsin all the way to Peking.

At the time there were a few co-workers who were waiting for me in Peking to travel together to Suiyuan, Shansi, and Shensi. Previously we had decided to preach the gospel in different provinces during the summer. Now that Japan had started the invasion of China, the co-workers and I felt that we should move quickly according to our original plan. We took the train from Peking to Suiyuan, and when we arrived in Suiyuan, we rode an open coach to Taiyuan, which is in Shansi. In Taiyuan we immediately started to meet and preach the gospel in every place. Next we went to Shensi and then went by train to Sian. In Sian we received a telegram from Brother Nee asking us to attend the co-worker's meeting in Hankow. We went from Sian through Chengchow to Hankow, and there we waited for Brother Nee. While waiting, I received the news that the Japanese army was about to take over Chefoo, so I had to return to Chefoo and get my family out. However, while I was on my way from Hankow to Chefoo, Chefoo was lost to the enemy, and I fell into the hands of the Japanese.

The next year I was arrested and put into prison. It was a short imprisonment, but some marvelous things happened. A few years later, at the end of 1942 and the beginning of 1943, a great revival began in Chefoo. We met continuously for almost one hundred days, and every day we had new leadings from the Lord. The brothers and sisters consecrated themselves to the extent that every individual and every home was consecrated, and they offered all their possessions, including house deeds, property deeds, stocks, and bank deposits. The serving ones were divided into groups to check and list all the material things offered by the saints. One group checked the garments, another group checked the jewelry, and still another group checked the utensils. They took turns to check and register all the items, one by one.

The news of this revival found its way to the Japanese army headquarters. The Japanese military police received an intelligence report leading them to suppose that in Chefoo there was a man with great charisma who had stirred up a group of people to the point that they gave up even their family possessions and delivered to him all their valuables. The Japanese military police said that apparently I was a preacher, but they had never seen such a phenomenon in Christianity. Therefore, they sent undercover workers disguised as saints to come and listen to the gospel. I knew the Japanese were watching me while I was speaking from the podium, so I cannot say that I was not concerned. On the one hand, I looked to the Lord, and on the other hand, I thought about the condition of Christianity. Born and raised in Christianity, I understood the situation of Christianity quite well. By that time I had worked with Brother Nee for nearly ten years, and I knew the Lord's truth was with us. Therefore, I had the thought within me, "O Lord, I cannot die." Where would the truths be if I died? I had only this one thought in mind: I could not die.

HAVING A DREAM OF A BROAD HIGHWAY

I rarely have dreams when I sleep, but I had a dream one night. In the dream I held a cane in my hand, walking peacefully until I came to a place with a steep, crooked downward slope with four steps. I went down the slope step by step, leaning on my cane, and suddenly a German shepherd dog threw itself on me. The German shepherd was the same color as that of the uniform of the Japanese military police. The German shepherd threw itself on me, but I was not wounded, and in an instant the dog went away. Suddenly, when I looked ahead, there was a broad highway very straight and stretching on boundlessly, and the sun had just risen from the east. My heart then felt free and released, and seeing the broad highway, the rising sun, and the boundless, bright horizon, I strode fearlessly onward. This was my dream.

The broad highway, the rising sun, and the boundless horizon greatly comforted me within. Through the dream the Lord told me, "Be at peace. You are not under the hand of the Japanese." The Japanese army was like the German shepherd attacking me, but eventually it could not hurt me. I knew that the Lord still wanted me to remain on the earth, because there was a broad highway ahead, and I could just keep going on.

Two or three weeks later, as usual, I went to the meeting hall before eight in the morning to take care of some things. As soon as I stepped into the meeting hall, there came two men dressed in blue Chinese long gowns. Right away I knew that one of them was Japanese and the other was a Chinese traitor as the interpreter. The Japanese officer said, "Mr. Lee, please excuse us. We are here to visit you." I welcomed them into the room which I used to pray and read the Bible. I had the Lord's leading within and gave him a pocket-sized Bible. In the end he told me, "I apologize, Mr. Lee, but we have to ask you to come to our headquarters. We have a few matters to discuss with you." I was then brought to the military police headquarters.

After I got there, they told me that they were very busy, and they asked me to be seated. I waited past lunchtime and dinnertime and was detained until nine or ten in the evening. Then they told me that it was late and that I should sleep overnight there and wait for the next day. At that time they did not put me in a prison cell right away but let me sleep on a bed belonging to a military policeman. That night I dreamed again: The German shepherd ran around me, harassing me, but because of the previous dream, I knew that it could not harm me. The next morning they brought me to the interrogation chamber where there were cold water and wooden boards. They made me lie on a wooden board, and then they poured cold water on me, into my mouth and nostrils and all over my body. Afterward, they gave me someone's name and asked if I knew that person. That person was a brother among us who had gone to Chungking from the inland a few months ago. They asked me where he was hiding. I said that I did not know. Then they asked me how he got there. I told them the church wrote a letter of recommendation for him. While they were interrogating me, I was looking to the Lord. For anything in which I could not reveal the truth, I would ask the Lord, "O Lord, do not let them ask me about it," and they truly did not ask at all. Whatever they asked, I was able to answer calmly and truthfully.

After the interrogation, they let me rest and then dragged me to the prison cell. Then they went to my house and the meeting hall to find the responsible ones to verify the statements I gave under interrogation. I was tortured in this way for more than three weeks. One night I had another dream. I dreamed that I was in a brother's home in my neighborhood, and a puppy crawled out of a dog hole, wagging its tail at me and running toward me. When I woke up I felt very happy and peaceful, because I knew that the Japanese military police were coming to me to "wag their tails" and send me home. At that time they interrogated me twice a day, for close to two or three hours each time. The next day, instead of interrogating they said to me, "Mr. Lee, we are young and impetuous. Please excuse us for any lack of respect." They wanted to escort me home, but they had to wait until the evening, so they treated me to a meal. The more they chattered, the more I felt they were like puppies wagging their tails.

The week after they sent me home, in the afternoon on the Lord's Day after I finished ministering the word, I sat down to partake of the Lord's table. When the bread and cup were passed to me, I had a trance similar to Peter's. In the trance I saw a white dog before me. This dog was not like the previous German shepherd or the hole-crawling puppy. I then realized that the Japanese were coming for me again.

As expected, after the Lord's Day they came again, requesting me to do a little work for them, saying that since I was a member of the church and had many contacts, I should help them investigate those who were Communists. This was difficult for me, since I did not know much. Besides, I would never do anything that would be harmful to my fellow countrymen. A week later, they came to ask me if I had any information for them. I said no. Another week later, I still answered no.

At the time I had to go to the Japanese military police and apply for entry and exit permits because I did not have the freedom to travel. However, I contracted a severe case of tuberculosis. After being ill for half a year, they received news of my illness and thought I was incapacitated and therefore useless, so they released me from their grasp. Thus, I escaped from the hands of the Japanese.

In October of 1944 I left Chefoo and fled to Tsingtao, where I recuperated for one and a half years. Japan surrendered in 1945, and shortly afterward the Communist army advanced into Chefoo. The first thing they did in Chefoo was to come to my home to look for me. All these events that occurred were evidences of the Lord's preserving me, enabling me to escape out of the hands of the Japanese and the Communists.

It has been over forty years since I first had the dream in 1943. After I had fully recovered from tuberculosis in 1946, the brothers in Shanghai and Nanking asked me to go there, so I went. That brought in a great revival. Then the political situation in mainland China became desperate, so Brother Nee and all the co-workers decided to send me overseas. I came to Taiwan and saw the Lord's blessing the whole time. Later, when I went to Southeast Asia, I again saw the Lord's blessing. Even after I went to the United States, the Lord's blessing was also evidently present. This is today's situation. I can say that every day I am walking on the broad highway, step by step. Especially today, seeing the development of this new way, it is truly a broad highway and a rising sun, with a boundless prospect. I really feel that this dream is still being fulfilled.

THE BROAD HIGHWAY OF THE LORD'S RECOVERY

As we look at today's world situation, review past history, observe the condition of Christianity, and consider the light shown to us in the Scriptures, it is not difficult to conclude that this is a critical moment in time. A British brother brought to me a copy of *The Times,* in which the statistics of Christianity in England are published: the Catholic Church has the most members, totaling 2.5 million; the Presbyterians also have 2.5 million. Beginning from 1970 the numbers dropped greatly. In 1990 the Catholic Church are expected to drop down to an estimated 1.8 million, while the Presbyterians are expected to drop down to an estimated 1.7 million. All the other denominations are in the process of losing members as well. However, in the list of statistics there is a group of Christians called the "home churches," which had not been in existence before 1970 but currently has eighty to ninety thousand members. This shows that the population of the whole of Christianity is decreasing all over the world. In other words, Christianity has no way, no future.

Supposedly Christianity has spread to the whole world. According to the numbers, however, in Taiwan there are less than five hundred thousand Christians in a total population of twenty million; therefore, the percentage of Christians is less than 2.5. This is to say that for every one hundred Taiwan residents, there are less than two and a half saved ones. The island of Taiwan has easy and convenient transportation, but Christianity has been here for more than two centuries without producing much result. Christianity all over the earth is in the same condition. Supposedly Christianity has been preached over the whole earth; in reality, it is low in number.

This certainly is a critical moment. Since the Lord has now shown us the new way and has called us to take the new way, we must keep up with Him. If the new way solely relies on the working saints to go out knocking on doors in their spare time, it will truly not be adequate. This way must rely on young, capable, and educated brothers and sisters receiving the burden to go full-time, serving the Lord every day and every hour. I hope that from this day onward the number of full-timers will increase year after year. This is the Lord's calling for us today.

I genuinely believe that the dream I had was a real vision. The past forty years that we have gone through proves that the dream has been fulfilled, and now we are still on this broad highway. At this point in time we particularly need young people to rise up and serve the Lord full-time. There is nothing more glorious than serving full-time. Consider this: The gaining of a million dollars cannot compare to the gaining of one soul. If we can spend several years to labor and save several thousand souls through door-knocking, and if they multiply continually, each bringing in new ones and establishing home meetings, and each maturing in life and learning the truth, how worthwhile it will be! This is the new way. This is the broad highway, the rising sun, and the boundless future.

(A message given in Taipei, Taiwan on May 23, 1987)

CHAPTER SEVEN

THE TREASURE OF THE UNIVERSE

THE WONDERFUL COMPOSITION OF THE EARTH

God created the universe with a center. In this universe there are many galaxies, the sun, the moon, and constellations, which constitute what we call heaven. Speaking from man's perspective, under the heaven is the earth. Therefore, man lives between heaven and earth. When scientists studied the moon, they discovered that it has no atmosphere around it. Therefore, there is no rain, and consequently the entire moon is incapable of growing life. According to scientific inference, life exists only on earth. Many parts of the earth are composed of minerals, which are essential to the existence of living things. For example, the elements of our human body are the same as the elements of dust, both being composed of minerals. Therefore, we need these minerals for our existence.

Moreover, the earth created by God in His wisdom is not only rich in minerals, but it also produces all kinds of living things. It first produces plants, including flowers, grass, and trees, which are in the principle of the "wood, grass, stubble" mentioned in 1 Corinthians 3:12. Plants are capable of propagating life. A seed, for example, after being buried in the ground brings forth many grains; this is the propagation of the seed.

Those who have been to Southeast Asia know that when the Chinese immigrated there to do business, they made money and became rich through planting rubber trees. They owned many acres of rubber plantations. The rubber that we use daily comes from these rubber trees. When a rubber tree has grown to a certain stage, latex seeps out if the bark is cut open. This latex from the rubber tree is the source of many rubber products such as washbasins, cups, and automobile tires, which are indispensable in our daily lives. This shows us that anything created by God, whether it is mineral, plant, or animal, can be used to produce something.

GOD DESIRING THAT THE REGENERATED MAN BE TRANSFORMED INTO PEARL AND PRECIOUS STONES

In God's creation, minerals, plants, and animals all undergo changes. Although God used clay to create human beings, He wants us to be transformed into pearl and precious stones. The way He transforms us is to continuously add His element of pure gold into us. We can become pearl and precious stones because we have His element of pure gold.

First Corinthians 3:9 says that the believers are God's cultivated land, God's farm, for growing plants, and it also says that the believers are God's building. This is truly wonderful in that it speaks first about a farm for growing plants and then about a building to be built with minerals. In verse 12, Paul first mentions gold, silver, and precious stones and then mentions wood, grass, and stubble, that is, first minerals, then plants. Paul also says that when a person's work is proved by fire, if it is in the nature of plants, it will be consumed. However, if it is built with gold, silver, and precious stones, his work is in the nature of minerals; it will remain, and he will receive a reward (vv. 13-14).

In summary, on this earth there are first minerals, and then plants are produced. It is apparent, however, that whether minerals or plants, they are either mostly dirt and rocks, or leaves and wood which are easily decomposed, and do not appear to be precious or valuable. They need to go through transformation to produce gold, pearl, and precious stones.

According to the record in Genesis 2, there is a kind of pearl that is produced out of the plant life (v. 12). In the New Testament, however, pearl is produced not out of the plant life but out of the animal life, out of oysters (Rev. 21:21). The pearl in Genesis 2 is produced by a resin producing plant, such as a rubber tree. When the life-juice that issues from this kind of tree is coagulated, it solidifies to become a pearl. However, the pearl mentioned in the New Testament is produced from oysters in the sea. When a grain of sand gets into an oyster, not only does it wound the oyster, but the foreign particle also stays within the oyster. When the grain of sand enters into the oyster, the oyster secretes its life-juice, which coats the grain of sand layer by layer. With each layer of coating the grain of sand becomes larger, and in the end it becomes a pearl.

CHRISTIANS HAVING A TREASURE WITHIN THEM FOR THE DIVINE BUILDING

In terms of life, the earth is the center of the universe. On the earth there are minerals and plants. Minerals consist mostly of dirt and sand, and plants are wood, grass, and stubble. Today as products of the earth, we are constituted with minerals and plants. The food we eat every day includes plants and minerals. In addition, we also eat animals, such as chicken, duck, fish, and beef. We human beings are compositions of these three kinds of substance. We are certainly very capable, because we not only can take in but also absorb all these things. After we have absorbed them, they become the elements of our body. Man's longevity depends on the body. A person with a healthy body lives a long life, while a person with an unhealthy body lives a short life. Regardless of how healthy a person is, if he does not eat or drink he will become sick and eventually die.

When a new human life is born, it weighs only about six or seven pounds. After a period of time it increases to twenty pounds, and after another period of time it may be over a hundred and thirty pounds. The reason human life has such a manifestation is that it is constituted with the elements of minerals, animals, and plants. Today, whether presidents, government heads, enterprisers, street sweepers, garbage collectors, whether college graduates, elementary school graduates, or uneducated persons, all are composed of dirt, sand, wood, grass, stubble, chicken, duck, fish, and beef. We can even say that they are heaps of all such materials.

We know that although jade, crystals, and other such things come from dirt and sand, they are gems and are precious. Today we who believe in Christ are composed of dirt, sand, wood, grass, stubble, chicken, duck, fish, and beef, but we are very different from people in the world, because we have a treasure inside of us. The treasure within us is none other than Christ (2 Cor. 4:7), who is God. Without God we are only compositions of minerals, plants, and animals; with God we have a precious element within us that makes us precious.

Even though the elements that make up the entire earth are nothing more than minerals (such as dirt and sand), plants (such as wood, grass, and stubble), and animals (such as chicken, duck, fish, and beef), we are different because we have God. First Peter 2:5 says that we are living stones, chosen and precious with God. We are precious living stones, and these living stones are not for exhibition but for the divine building. Isaiah 28:16 says, "Therefore thus says / The Lord Jehovah: Indeed I lay a stone in Zion / ...A precious cornerstone." This cornerstone indicates building. Therefore, in the church we are not like the items in a jewelry store that are only for display. Rather, every day we are growing and being transformed for the building of God.

In the Gospel of John the Lord tells us that He is the true vine (15:1). This means that all the other vines are not real; only the Lord Himself is the true vine. Since He is the true vine, we are joined to Him as the same vine; the only difference is that He is the root, the source, and we are the branches (v. 5). We know that a tree with only the root or trunk but without any branches is not a complete tree. Christ and we are the vine that bears fruit. The fruit that we bear is the outflow of life. When life flows out from the plant, it becomes pearl. Therefore, on the one hand we are dirt, sand, wood, grass, and stubble; but on the other hand we are filled with the element of gold. God as gold is in us to transform us into pearl and precious stones for His building. In other words, God's building is built with these precious materials. The building composed of these materials is the greatest treasure in the universe.

PREACHING THE GOSPEL WITH BOLDNESS

As saved ones, we have truly been blessed with God's special grace, so we should go and preach the gospel everywhere. We should go knock on the doors of the president, the cabinet heads, and the college deans. Some may say that these doors are not easy to knock on because they are doors of people of high position and influence who will not open their doors to us. If that is the case, we can use the telephone. If they will not pick up the telephone, we can write letters. When going out to contact people, we have at least three ways: knocking on doors, making telephone calls, and writing letters. In addition, we can send books such as gospel pamphlets by mail. If we are faithful in our practice, in all these ways there will be one that works.

We have to tell people that whether they are the head of a nation, the head of a government department, or the head of a university, one day all of these "heads" will pass away and vanish, and all that will remain is dirt, sand, and other elements. There is a brother among us who went through the Whampoa Military Academy and was a high ranking military officer. Nevertheless, today he is no longer any kind of "head." Happily, he believes in the Lord Jesus. If he did not believe, he would be left with only the elements of animals, plants, and minerals, and one day when he closes his eyes and expires, all that he has will come to an end, and he will have nothing.

Whether a person occupies the highest position or works as a street vendor, the outcome is the same. That is why we ought to preach the gospel to people, telling them that regardless of their occupation today, in the end they will be only a pile of mineral, plant, and animal elements; there will not be much left. Some of us are younger and some of us are older; the difference is only a matter of time, eighty years at the most. Eventually, the older ones will be the first ones to turn into a pile of dust, and the younger ones will also follow suit to be dust. There is no difference in their end.

THE EXCELLENT CHOICE IN HUMAN LIFE

Today by the Lord's mercy we have made a high choice,

which is also an excellent choice. I was saved at the age of nineteen in 1925. That afternoon I heard the gospel in a large chapel, and I was very clear that I was saved. Before then I was born and raised in Christianity, but I was not a believer. Furthermore, because of the Chinese ethical education that I had received, I greatly despised Christianity and its practices. I considered it a religion preached by foreigners who could only teach that sinners would go to hell and good people would go to heaven. To me, such teaching was far too inferior when compared with Chinese Confucian philosophy.

Yet that afternoon the Lord caught me under very special circumstances. The sister who preached the gospel was only six years older than I was. That day she did not talk about hell or heaven, nor did she talk about bad people or good people. She was from the Yangtze River valley in the south and was serving in the region around Shanghai. Rarely did she come up to the north, but in 1925 she was invited by the denominations to come and preach the gospel in my home-town, Chefoo. I had always attended Christian schools and had been accustomed to the so-called sermons and gospel, and I was even getting tired of them. During my childhood, because the school was next to the chapel, every Lord's Day morning the teachers would have us line up one by one and would take us to the chapel to hear the pastors speak. I was weary of listening to them, especially because they did not speak fluent Mandarin Chinese. Therefore, I did not have a good impression whenever Christianity or the church was mentioned.

Because of my family's Christian background, outwardly I would nevertheless argue for and defend Christianity. I remember that every time the school took us on a field trip, whenever we passed by a temple a classmate would bring up questions concerning God, and I would argue with him, tell-ing him that all those idols are false and that only the God we have in Christianity is real. Even though I said such things, I myself did not believe. It was extremely self-contradictory. Back then I always felt that going to operas, playing soccer, and playing games were far more exciting and interesting than attending church meetings.

However, on that day when I heard that a twenty-five year old woman from Shanghai would be preaching the gospel to us, I thought it was quite extraordinary. From my youth I had never heard a woman preaching the gospel, so I went and listened to her speaking. This sister truly had the presence of the Lord. She told the story of the Israelites' exodus from Egypt. She said that Pharaoh typifies the devil, Satan, whose main intention is to usurp men with the "Egyptian" world. She spoke with great power, and I was caught immediately. I then prayed to the Lord, "Lord, I do not want this world. I do not want to be usurped by Satan. I want God Himself." With this inward feeling, I prayed as I listened to the speaking onstage until the meeting ended.

Sixty years ago the meetings in the denominations were such that when the meeting was dismissed, the atmosphere was quite cold. There were no after-meeting conversations, and no one would come to contact you. Generally speaking, after a church service, everyone would simply go home separately, and no one bothered anyone else. Therefore, we could attend services for ten years without ever having a real conversation with anyone. After the meeting was dismissed that day, while I was walking alone, I was full of feeling in my heart and knew that I was saved. I still remember that on my way home when I came to a street corner, I stopped, stood still, and prayed to God a prayer that I can never forget. I prayed, "O God, even if the whole earth is given to me, and even if the entire world asks me to be king, I would not accept it. I just want You."

We all need to make the best choice. Even if a person becomes the president of a nation or the principal of a school, in the end he is nothing more than a pile of dust, sand, wood, and other elements. According to the apostle Paul, all human attainments are merely refuse (Phil. 3:7-8). Only when we gain God, when we gain Christ, have we made the best choice.

When I entered to study at a junior college, I was clear in my heart that even if I did well in my studies I did not study for study's sake. At that time I did not know about consecration, and no one told me about consecration. Still, walking on the road one day I spontaneously told God, "O God, some day

I will carry a Bible bag and preach the gospel in all the villages and small towns. Even if I have to drink from mountain brooks and live on tree roots, I am willing to do anything as long as I can preach the gospel, and I will be satisfied." I did not understand much Bible truth at the time, but I had this thought within me, that apart from pursuing and gaining the Lord, everything else in human life does not matter.

Therefore, if we would choose the Lord and spend time learning to serve Him, we have made the super-choice, the excellent choice. Today the environment of the church is an environment of "gold, silver, precious stones." Most of us have received a higher education, and in the church life we are also immersed in the word of God, in God Himself. This enables us to grow and be transformed in life daily. Regardless of how long we have been in the church life, I believe that we all have the same feeling that we are growing, God's golden nature is also growing within us, and that there is transformation within us. Ultimately, we will be built together. We are not individual precious stones or pearls, but we are being built with one another.

THE TREASURE OF THE UNIVERSE

Today we have a part in God's building. Individually, we are each a pearl and a precious stone. Corporately, we should be a collective entity of gold, silver, precious stones, and pearl. This is the church today, and in the future it will ultimately consummate in the New Jerusalem. This is the treasure of the universe, the desire of God's heart.

God created the universe and the earth for the producing of the church. First, the saints are produced through the redemption of Christ. Next, the church is constituted with the saints. Lastly, the constituted church is enlarged to consummate in the New Jerusalem. At that point the New Jerusalem will still be on the earth, but the earth will have become the new heaven and new earth. It will be a new earth, but it will still be the earth. God is very interested in the earth, because it is on the earth that He will produce the saints and build the church, which eventually will be enlarged to become the New Jerusalem.

Everything is a treasure in the New Jerusalem. The description in the Bible is very clear. It says that the city proper is a mountain of pure gold (Rev. 21:18). The foundations of the wall of the city are all precious stones, with at least twelve different kinds of stones (vv. 19-20). In addition, this city has twelve gates, each composed of one pearl (v. 21). Therefore, this city is truly a city of pure gold, precious stones, and pearl, which is the aggregate of the mingling of the processed Triune God with His chosen, redeemed, regenerated, and transformed tripartite man. Ultimately, the Triune God will take us as His dwelling place, and we will take Him as our dwelling place. Thus He and we will live together for eternity. This is the story of the universal treasure. Today our choice is excellent, our human life is excellent, the meaning of our human life is excellent, and the goal of our human life is excellent. Eventually what we attain to in our human life will be even more excellent; it will be unparalleled.

We are fortunate to be people who have God and who have a vision. We see ourselves as pearls and precious stones, not a pile of dirt and sand, nor a pile of wood, grass, and stubble, neither a pile of chicken, duck, fish, and beef. We are a building constituted with precious stones and pearl. Our human life is excellent, the meaning of our human life is excellent, and the purpose of our human life is excellent. This purpose is none other than the mingling of God and man. God wants to mingle Himself with us, who are men of clay, to transform us completely into precious stones and pearl.

Today we all are being transformed, growing, and being built together. This is the church, today's treasure and tomorrow's New Jerusalem. One day in the New Jerusalem we will not see a single piece of wood or stone. Rather, everything will be pure gold, precious stones, and pearl. Today we should have the same expression. This is the treasure of the universe.

(A message given in the Full-Time Training in Taipei, Taiwan on April 11, 1990)

CHAPTER EIGHT

THE MINISTERS AND THE MINISTRY
OF THE NEW TESTAMENT

Scripture Reading: 2 Cor. 3:6, 8; Col. 1:27-29; Eph. 3:8-10; 4:11-13; 2 Cor. 4:1-2, 5

The ministry of the New Testament serving ones (ministers) is to announce Christ and to dispense and minister Christ with His riches to people to produce the local churches for the building up of the universal Body of Christ as the expression of the Triune God.

THE MINISTERS AND THE MINISTRY

Recently, after several trainings the Lord has truly graced us in every way, and He truly has spoken to us, clearly revealing to us the new way that He wants us to take. I treasure this opportunity to have fellowship with you before I depart. I offer you the above verses as a farewell gift. I hope you will digest these verses in accordance with the spirit of the training, allowing this word to mingle with you in a marvelous way.

These verses mainly show us the ministers and the ministry of the New Testament. *Ministers* refers to persons, whereas *ministry* refers to the work. These two aspects are revealed in the New Testament, especially in the Epistles of the apostle Paul, for our attention. The first aspect is that God in His grace, through His redemption, and by His Spirit has raised up a group of people who love Him, who are willing to forsake everything for Him, and who set apart their time to serve Him. In the New Testament they are called ministers. A minister is one who serves. We who are called by the Lord are those who serve the Lord. Apparently, we serve men; actually, we serve the Lord. With what do we serve men? We serve today's thirsty ones with Christ, with the gospel, with truth, with grace, and with the life supply. Therefore, we are the Lord's serving ones. Such ones are ministers.

The other aspect is the ministry. The ministry is the one work we all are doing and the one commission we all bear together. In other words, *ministers* refers to us, the persons, while *ministry* refers to the commission we bear, the work we do.

THE CONTENT AND THE GOAL
OF THE WORK OF THE MINISTRY

What is the work of the ministry? This work is to announce to people the unsearchable riches of Christ (Eph. 3:8), and to enlighten all that they may see the mystery which has been hidden in God, who created all things (v. 9), in order that they may understand, accept, and together receive grace, resulting in the producing of the church. On the positive side, God uses the church for our perfecting. On the negative side, through the church God will make known His multifarious wisdom to the heavens, Satan, and all the fallen angels under Satan's command (v. 10).

Ephesians 3:8 through 10 clearly shows us that we who are called by God, who bear God's commission, and who do the work of Christ, on the one hand, have to supply people with the unsearchable riches of Christ, and on the other hand, we have to enlighten all that they may see the mystery, which throughout the ages has been hidden in God, who created all things. The end, the final goal, is that through the preaching of the truth people will be raised up to produce the church so that the church may be expressed in every place, that people may receive grace and be perfected, making known the multifarious wisdom of God to Satan and the fallen angels.

THE GRACE OF GOD ENABLING MAN TO DO
THE WORK OF THE MINISTRY

To do the work of the ministry requires the grace of God. We cannot do this work by ourselves. This work is different from any common work because it is dealing not with any kind of philosophy or doctrine but with the mystery hidden in God. The work of the ministry is to announce to people the unsearchable riches of Christ and to enlighten them that they may see the hidden mystery of God, and to produce the church for perfecting people to make known the multifarious wisdom of God. We cannot do this work by our natural ability or by acquired learning. Rather, we need the grace of God.

Regarding this grace, we may suppose that only the apostle Paul was able to receive it and that since we are smaller than Paul, we are not qualified. However, in Ephesians 3:8 Paul told us that he was less than the least of all saints. This indicates that since Paul was able to receive such grace, every one of us who is saved can also receive the same grace. When we have this grace, we can go forth with Christ and be full of light to make known the mystery of God. Our going to every nation is to announce the riches of Christ to people and to reveal to them the mystery of God that the churches may be produced in every nation and in every place. This is what the grace of God enables us to do. I believe that in the coming days the grace of God will be with us more abundantly, causing us to do the same work that Paul did.

ANNOUNCING THE LIVING CHRIST TO PEOPLE BY OPENING UP THE REVELATIONS IN THE BIBLE

We do not go out to preach a religion, nor do we go to preach any philosophy or doctrine. We preach Jesus Christ, the living God and Savior. He is the embodiment of the Triune God. He became flesh, passed through human living, and went to the cross to die for our sins, resurrected, and became the life-giving Spirit. He is present everywhere; He goes everywhere; He penetrates everywhere. Wherever a person is, if he is willing to open himself and call on the Lord's name, the Lord as the Spirit will enter into him like fresh air, causing him to receive Christ Himself.

This is the Christ we preach. We do not preach religion, nor even the so-called biblical truths alone. Rather, we open up the revelations in the Bible to people. Revelation means the raising of the curtain, the opening of the veil, the uncovering of a previously hidden object. For example, if I button up my jacket, you will have no idea what is hidden under it. Then I may unfold the lapels of my jacket; this is to uncover, to unveil, for you to see the tie I have under my jacket. This is to "enlighten all," as mentioned in Ephesians 3:9. This is the work we do when we go out to visit people—ministering Christ to people and releasing the truth that they may be enlightened and be able to see the mystery which has been hidden in God throughout the ages.

Ephesians 4:11 and 12 continues, "And He Himself gave some as apostles and some as prophets and some as evangelists and some as shepherds and teachers, for the perfecting of the saints unto the work of the ministry, unto the building up of the Body of Christ." Today in the church there are many such gifts. Some are apostles, some are prophets, some are evangelists, and some are shepherds and teachers. The work they do is to perfect the saints. For instance, a full-time serving one goes out door-knocking to preach the gospel, and after some have been saved, he meets with them in their homes for their perfecting. In this way, they can do the work that we all do, which is to announce Christ, make known the mystery of God, and establish the local churches, that is, building up the Body of Christ.

Furthermore, in 2 Corinthians 4:1 and 2 Paul says, "Therefore, having this ministry as we have been shown mercy, we do not lose heart; but we have renounced the hidden things of shame, not walking in craftiness nor adulterating the word of God, but by the manifestation of the truth." This means that as we have received God's commission and bear God's entrustment to preach Christ to people and release the truth concerning the mystery of God to them, we need to have a good expression, a proper living, before men. This will cause us to not lose heart but to renounce the shameful, unmentionable, and hidden things and not walk in craftiness. All of us who serve the Lord full-time should be absolutely honest, without the slightest bit of falsehood or deceit. In this way we will be able to manifest the truth of God. This is concerning the proper character that we need.

The point we have been emphasizing is that we all should know that we do not go out merely to be the so-called preachers or evangelists. Rather, we are people who have Christ—and even are filled with Him—in our spirit. We even let our lives be saturated and filled with this living Lord, this pneumatic Christ. It is with such a Lord that we go out to preach the gospel, and we preach not only the truth of the gospel, but all the more we preach this living Christ as the center of the gospel.

THE WAY TO RECEIVE SALVATION

Furthermore, we need to see that when we believe in Christ, we do not have a change of religion, whether from Buddhism to Christianity, that is, from one certain religion to another. Converting from one religion to another is not faith in Christ. Rather, we have to open ourselves in our heart and spirit, which is where our real person is, and receive the true and living Savior, the Creator of heaven and earth, the Savior who bled and died for us, and the One who has become the life-giving Spirit. It is such a One that we have to receive into us. How do we receive Him? The way to receive Him is very simple; it does not require us to do anything, and it does not even require deep consideration. Wherever we may be, if we open our whole being and pray to Jesus Christ, He will come into us. Romans 10:13 says, "Whoever calls upon the name of the Lord shall be saved." He is such a living Savior; like fresh air, He is waiting to enter into those who open to Him.

We all know that when a person opens his mouth and takes a deep breath, he can receive an abundance of fresh air. Today we need only to say, "O Lord Jesus, I am a sinner. Thank You, You are not only my Creator, but You also died for me on the cross to become my Redeemer. Lord, I receive You. Please come into me." Every one of us can try touching the Lord like this. If we faithfully open ourselves in this way, calling on the Lord from the depths of our spirit, we will see that from then on our lives will have a gradual change from our inner heart to our outward behavior. This is not a change as a result of man's teaching, but it is the Lord in us as the true and living life that causes us to have a change in life through a metabolic process of life. This is a mystery, yet it is clearly revealed in the Bible.

Today all parts of the world lack this truth. Since we are in the Lord's recovery, we ought to bear this commission and go to all parts of the world to speak and explain to people the mysterious truth concerning this living Jesus. By the Christ who lives in us we release Christ that He may enter into people as fresh air. Thus, people will not only be saved but also love God, and the more they love God, the more they will love one another. This loving of one another will stir up in them a desire to gather together in the Lord's name. This gathering together is the church. In the beginning they may be few in number, but as long as they continue to come together, like burning coals of fire burning together they will become more and more burning. We all know that if we put some pieces of coal or wood together and kindle them, they will burn one another. This piece burns that piece, and that piece burns this piece; eventually all will be burning. However, a single piece of wood or coal does not burn readily but instead dies out easily. We need to come together as the church called out by God that we may receive grace to be perfected by God and be used by Him to manifest His multifarious wisdom.

This is my parting word to the full-time trainees. May the Lord be with you all, that regardless of which country or place you return to, you will have Christ accompanying you, and you will also have the truth of God filling you within, so that wherever you are, what is expressed in your living and your conduct is not any sinful, corrupted thing, nor yourself, but the living Christ, the shining Christ. May the Lord be with your spirit. Amen.

(A message given in the graduation meeting of the Full-Time Training in Taipei, Taiwan on June 1, 1987)

ABOUT THE AUTHOR

Witness Lee was born in 1905 in northern China and raised in a Christian family. At age 19 he was fully captured for Christ and immediately consecrated himself to preach the gospel for the rest of his life. Early in his service, he met Watchman Nee, a renowned preacher, teacher, and writer. Witness Lee labored together with Watchman Nee under his direction. In 1934 Watchman Nee entrusted Witness Lee with the responsibility for his publication operation, called the Shanghai Gospel Bookroom.

Prior to the Communist takeover in 1949, Witness Lee was sent by Watchman Nee and his other co-workers to Taiwan to insure that the things delivered to them by the Lord would not be lost. Watchman Nee instructed Witness Lee to continue the former's publishing operation abroad as the Taiwan Gospel Bookroom, which has been publicly recognized as the publisher of Watchman Nee's works outside China. Witness Lee's work in Taiwan manifested the Lord's abundant blessing. From a mere 350 believers, newly fled from the mainland, the churches in Taiwan grew to 20,000 in five years.

In 1962 Witness Lee felt led of the Lord to come to the United States, settling in California. During his 35 years of service in the U.S., he ministered in weekly meetings and weekend conferences, delivering several thousand spoken messages. Much of his speaking has since been published as over 400 titles. Many of these have been translated into over fourteen languages. He gave his last public conference in February 1997 at the age of 91.

He leaves behind a prolific presentation of the truth in the Bible. His major work, *Life-study of the Bible,* comprises over 25,000 pages of commentary on every book of the Bible from the perspective of the believers' enjoyment and experience of God's divine life in Christ through the Holy Spirit. Witness Lee was the chief editor of a new translation of the New Testament into Chinese called the Recovery Version and directed the translation of the same into English. The Recovery Version also appears in a number of other languages. He provided an extensive body of footnotes, outlines, and spiritual cross references. A radio broadcast of his messages can be heard on Christian radio stations in the United States. In 1965 Witness Lee founded Living Stream Ministry, a non-profit corporation, located in Anaheim, California, which officially presents his and Watchman Nee's ministry.

Witness Lee's ministry emphasizes the experience of Christ as life and the practical oneness of the believers as the Body of Christ. Stressing the importance of attending to both these matters, he led the churches under his care to grow in Christian life and function. He was unbending in his conviction that God's goal is not narrow sectarianism but the Body of Christ. In time, believers began to meet simply as the church in their localities in response to this conviction. In recent years a number of new churches have been raised up in Russia and in many eastern European countries.

OTHER BOOKS PUBLISHED BY
Living Stream Ministry

Titles by Witness Lee:

Abraham—Called by God	0-7363-0359-6
The Experience of Life	0-87083-417-7
The Knowledge of Life	0-87083-419-3
The Tree of Life	0-87083-300-6
The Economy of God	0-87083-415-0
The Divine Economy	0-87083-268-9
God's New Testament Economy	0-87083-199-2
The World Situation and God's Move	0-87083-092-9
Christ vs. Religion	0-87083-010-4
The All-inclusive Christ	0-87083-020-1
Gospel Outlines	0-87083-039-2
Character	0-87083-322-7
The Secret of Experiencing Christ	0-87083-227-1
The Life and Way for the Practice of the Church Life	0-87083-785-0
The Basic Revelation in the Holy Scriptures	0-87083-105-4
The Crucial Revelation of Life in the Scriptures	0-87083-372-3
The Spirit with Our Spirit	0-87083-798-2
Christ as the Reality	0-87083-047-3
The Central Line of the Divine Revelation	0-87083-960-8
The Full Knowledge of the Word of God	0-87083-289-1
Watchman Nee—A Seer of the Divine Revelation ...	0-87083-625-0

Titles by Watchman Nee:

How to Study the Bible	0-7363-0407-X
God's Overcomers	0-7363-0433-9
The New Covenant	0-7363-0088-0
The Spiritual Man 3 volumes	0-7363-0269-7
Authority and Submission	0-7363-0185-2
The Overcoming Life	1-57593-817-0
The Glorious Church	0-87083-745-1
The Prayer Ministry of the Church	0-87083-860-1
The Breaking of the Outer Man and the Release ...	1-57593-955-X
The Mystery of Christ	1-57593-954-1
The God of Abraham, Isaac, and Jacob	0-87083-932-2
The Song of Songs	0-87083-872-5
The Gospel of God 2 volumes	1-57593-953-3
The Normal Christian Church Life	0-87083-027-9
The Character of the Lord's Worker	1-57593-322-5
The Normal Christian Faith	0-87083-748-6
Watchman Nee's Testimony	0-87083-051-1

Available at
Christian bookstores, or contact Living Stream Ministry
2431 W. La Palma Ave. • Anaheim, CA 92801
1-800-549-5164 • www.livingstream.com